THE
RENAISSANCE

SIX ESSAYS, by

Wallace K. Ferguson

Robert S. Lopez

George Sarton

Roland H. Bainton

Leicester Bradner

Erwin Panofsky

HARPER TORCHBOOKS

THE ACADEMY LIBRARY

HARPER & ROW PUBLISHERS

NEW YORK AND EVANSTON

THE
RENAISSANCE

PREFACE

There can be no question that one may approach the art of any period as a purely aesthetic experience without regard for the human element involved. In other words, one may contemplate an art object without inquiring as to its content, or the forces that brought it forth, or the circumstances that moulded it into its final form. But it is equally true that the more we relate any artistic manifestation to the many facets of human existence, the more the art becomes alive, suffused with vitality, and comprehensible to the beholder. Such an insight into the background does not detract from the aesthetic enjoyment, but, on the contrary, enhances it to a marked degree. In an effort to present this point of view to the public, three symposia were held at The Metropolitan Museum of Art during the winter of 1951-1952. On each of these occasions, five speakers devoted themselves to the cultural background of a given period, sketching it from different points of view—historical, economic, religious, social, and literary. Only when this task had been accomplished was the art, as the outgrowth of these factors, considered by the sixth member of the panel.

Because the first symposium, The Age of Diocletian, covered a fairly definite span of time and was confined to the Roman Empire, little difficulty was experienced in focusing the papers on the subject at hand. In the case of the Renaissance, the problem was much more complex, for the panel had to deal with an epoch in history rather than the reign of one emperor, with the developments in a number of countries rather than those in one empire. But there was a further complication. It appeared quite impossible to reach any decision as to the historical limits of this period, or, indeed, to agree on a definition of the Renaissance itself. This confusion is certain to shock those of the older school brought up on Burckhardt; yet the final result, as the following papers so clearly demonstrate, proved to be most stimulating and instructive.

It is, therefore, the pleasant duty of the Museum to thank most sincerely the six notable scholars whose papers are, by their kind permission, here presented as delivered.* Unfortunately, it proved to be impossible to include the discussion of questions raised by members of the panel and those submitted from 'the floor after the close of each lecture. Nevertheless, the articles in themselves are certain to be read with enjoyment and profit by laymen and students alike.

* Dr. Panofsky has revised his essay for the Torchbook edition.

CONTENTS

List of Illustrations

I TOWARD THE MODERN STATE

by Wallace K. Ferguson

In this symposium we shall discuss a crucial period in the history of western civilization. Broadly interpreted, the age of Diocletian marked a decisive stage in the transition from the classical, the Greco-Roman, civilization of the ancient Roman Empire to the Christian-Germanic civilization of the early Middle Ages. Similarly interpreted, the age of the Renaissance marked the transition from the fully developed civilization of the Middle Ages to the modern world. In planning these symposia,[1] the directors of the Metropolitan Museum have followed, whether consciously or not, a notable precedent. Nearly a hundred years ago, that great pioneer in the field of cultural history, Jacob Burckhardt, chose these two periods for his most significant historical works. In the first of these, *The Age of Constantine the Great*, published in 1852,[2] his aim, as expressed in the preface, was "to portray the half century from the rise of Diocletian to the death of Constantine in its peculiar character as an age of transition." In the second, *The Civilization of the Renaissance in Italy*, published in 1860,[3] he strove to analyze the spirit of Italian culture in the age which he considered to be the birth hour of the modern world. And in both works Burckhardt undertook, as we shall undertake in these discussions, a topical treatment of the various aspects of the civilization in question, beginning with the political background.

The introduction of Burckhardt's name at this point is

[1] See preface, p. v.
[2] Now available in an Anchor paperback edition.
[3] Now available in a Harper Torchbook edition, 1958.

not entirely irrelevant, nor is it inspired solely by the piety
that would have us praise famous men and our fathers that
begat us. It is, in fact, difficult to discuss the interpretation of the Renaissance without mentioning Burckhardt.
Wherever two or three Renaissance scholars are gathered
together his name keeps cropping up in the conversation—
like King Charles's head. For Burckhardt was not only a
great Renaissance historian; he was also, in a sense, the
creator of the Renaissance considered as a period in the history of European civilization. And almost all the historians
of the Renaissance since his time have taken his work as a
starting point and have labored to amplify, modify, or
reject his interpretation of the age. Thanks to the impres-
sion made by his great essay, historians remained for a long
time in a happy state of agreement concerning the general
character, cultural content, and chronological scope of the
Renaissance. When they talked about the Renaissance, however much they might disagree in matters of detail, they
were at least talking about the same phenomenon. Their
Renaissance was Burckhardt's, even when it was carried
across the Alps and naturalized somewhat uneasily in the
northern countries. But that idyllic condition no longer
exists. In recent years the traditional conception of the
Renaissance which Burckhardt crystallized has been
modified so drastically and in so many different ways that it
has become all things to all men. Some scholars would even
deny that it ever existed. That such variety of interpretation
was inevitable, and possibly even desirable, Burckhardt himself recognized. In the Introduction to *The Civilization of
the Renaissance in Italy*, he wrote:

> To each eye, perhaps, the outlines of a given civilization
> present a different picture; and in treating of a civilization
> which is the mother of our own, and whose influence is
> still at work among us, it is unavoidable that individual
> judgment and feeling should tell every moment both on
> the writer and on the reader. In the wide ocean upon

which we venture the possible ways and directions are many; and the same studies which have served for this work might easily, in other hands, not only receive a wholly different treatment and application, but lead also to essentially different conclusions.[4]

I may add that this prophetic intuition has been amply borne out by experience. I need not, however, labor further the point that historians have not always interpreted the Renaissance in the same way. It will probably become obvious enough as our symposium proceeds. Nor shall I attempt to outline for you all the conflicting tendencies of interpretation that have characterized Renaissance scholarship during the past half century.[5] As a German friend once said to me in reply to an innocent question concerning the nature of existentialist philosophy, "That is something you are as well without knowing anything about off." I mention the subject only because I feel that I should warn you not to be surprised if my learned colleagues should prove not to be in entire agreement concerning the character or even the chronological scope of the Renaissance. My own problem, if not altogether simple, is at least relatively uncontroversial. I shall here present some aspects of the political background of the Renaissance, and most historians would agree that in this field the development of greatest significance during the period was the emergence of states of a modern type, though not all would agree with the dates I assign to that development, nor with my conception of its causes.

The Renaissance, it seems to me, was, in a peculiar way, an age of transition. Every age is, of course, more or less transitional, since it is the nature of history to be constantly changing. The fleeting present is ever the transitional link through which all our yesterdays flow uninterruptedly into

[4] J. Burckhardt, *The Civilization of the Renaissance in Italy*, Harper Torchbook edition, 1958, p. 1.
[5] For a review of these see W. K. Ferguson, *The Renaissance in Historical Thought*, Boston, 1948.

the infinite succession of tomorrow and tomorrow and tomorrow. But there are few periods in the history of western
civilization—I would venture to say not more than two, unless our own age should prove to be a third—in which the
transition from the preceding to the following age makes so
complete a transformation that it may be regarded as a
change in kind rather than in degree. Such a change was
involved in the transition from medieval to modern civilization. And the Renaissance owes much of its peculiar character, I think, to the uneasy coexistence within it of medieval and modern elements, of decaying or obsolescent institutions and ways of thinking, together with new institutions
and ideas still imperfectly formed. For the history of political
institutions, the first decisive stage in the transition may be
dated from about the beginning of the fourteenth century.
The process was virtually complete by the end of the sixteenth
century. We have then a period of roughly three hundred
years to consider.

Unfortunately, we cannot limit our discussion to those three
hundred years, long though that period is. The causes and
the character of the changes that took place in the transitional
period cannot be made clear without some description of the
political institutions of the Middle Ages. Briefly stated, the
predominant factor in medieval political life was that mud-
dled complex of personal relations, private jurisdictions, and
local particularism known to us as the feudal system. This
was a method of organizing government, evolved out of
that necessity which is the mother of invention, during the
early Middle Ages, at a time when there was little regular
commerce, when normal city life had almost disappeared, and
when all classes depended for their living largely on the
cultivation of the soil, either directly as workers or indirectly
as landholders. From this economic situation two facts emerge
which have a direct bearing on the formation of feudal government: first, the fact that land represented the only considerable form of wealth and, second, the fact that, since each

rural community was to a large extent self-sufficient, there was little need for money as a medium of exchange and hence very little money in circulation. Services of any kind could therefore be paid for, as a rule, only by grants of land; and, conversely, rent for the use of land could be paid only by services, whether manual, religious, or military. Allowing for the inconvenient exceptions that partially vitiate any generalization about medieval society, the exchange of land for services prevailed from top to bottom of the feudal system, including the manorial organization which was its economic base. And this exchange involved a personal relation between the grantor of the land and the tenant, which on both sides tended to become hereditary. The king was thus forced to grant land in fief to great lords in payment for military service and for the administration of justice and the maintenance of law and order. Lacking the monetary revenue to maintain these essential functions of government, the king could scarcely do otherwise. The lords who thus became his vassals-in-chief in their turn granted parts of their land to vassals of their own on similar terms, and for similar reasons. That, at least, is the feudal theory. In actual practice what probably happened was that landholders of all grades usurped the functions and exercised the authority of government on their own lands because they alone were in a position to do so. And if they held their land in tenure rather than free ownership and did military service for it, they did so because they needed protection, because they felt a vague need for a legal theory to bolster their *de facto* power, and because society could not have been held together in any other way. The result of the process, at any rate, was the decentralization of government and the dismemberment of the state into a host of private jurisdictions. As stated by feudal lawyers, the basic principle of government was that every baron is sovereign in his own barony.

Needless to say, this system implied a severe curtailment of the king's authority and at times, as in tenth and eleventh century France, it came close to destroying his authority entirely. The king was the ultimate feudal lord, the apex of the feudal pyramid, but in practice he could exercise direct authority only over those lords who held their land directly from him. A chain of command ran downward from the king to the smallest *seigneurie*, but the chain was no stronger than its weakest link, and few would bear any great strain. Nevertheless, even in the most chaotic period of feudalism, the king was still the king, that is, he was something more than a suzerain to whom vassals as powerful as himself owed a vague obedience. Some imponderable element of prestige clung to the royal title. There was a kind of divinity that did hedge even a feudal king. He was the Lord's anointed, consecrated at his coronation as was Saul by the prophet Samuel. The monarchy thus survived until a change in the economic situation made possible the re-establishment of effective central government.

Signs of the economic change that would eventually produce that result began to appear in the eleventh century, or as Mr. Lopez would argue,[6] as early as the tenth century. Commerce began to revive in western Europe and introduced a new era of expanding prosperity. Throughout the twelfth and thirteenth centuries interregional trade grew steadily in volume; old cities came back to life and new cities were founded; a growing urban population of merchants and skilled craftsmen exchanged goods with the surrounding countryside; and money began to circulate more and more freely as buying and selling gradually replaced barter and rents, and wages began to take the place of tenures and labor services. Kings began to enjoy larger revenues and used the power of money to expand the scope of their government. But the feudal system did not wither away in proportion as the conditions which had made it necessary disappeared. The independence and the private jurisdictions which the land-

[6] R. Lopez, "Still another Renaissance," *The American Historical Review*, LVII (1951), pp. 1-21.

holding class had acquired during the early feudal period were now sanctioned by generations of custom and precedent. They were sanctioned still further by the universal prevalence of feudal ways of thinking from which even kings were not immune. Medieval men thought of government in terms of feudal relations as naturally as we think of it in terms of democracy and citizenship. Moreover, the king's ability to increase his revenue was strictly limited by the nature of the feudal contract between himself and his vassals, the form of which had been fixed at a time when money was unavailable. The king's vassals owed him military service and certain occasional aids, but no regular taxes; and the king could not go over their heads to tax their dependents without infringing upon their sovereign rights in their own fiefs.

There was a limit then to the extent to which the central government of the state could augment either its revenue or its effective authority within the framework of the feudal system. And by the end of the thirteenth century that limit had been reached in both France and England and to a lesser extent in the other kingdoms and principalities of western Europe. Any further development of royal power would necessitate a breach with the fundamental concepts of feudal government, and further development was inevitable. The change to a money economy from an economy founded on land and services strengthened the monarchy while it weakened the nobility, and that change was destined to continue with increasing rapidity. Loosely organized though it seemed to be, the feudal system possessed a certain tough vitality that enabled it to absorb the alien economic force of money for more than two centuries without apparently fatal results, but by the end of the thirteenth century it had reached the saturation point. From that time on, the economic foundations on which feudalism rested were in the last stages of disintegration and the structure reared upon them could not long endure.

The general tendencies which were common to all western

European countries were, of course, modified and conditioned by the particular political circumstances prevailing in each state. Only in France and England did the feudal state evolve directly into national monarchy. In Germany the imperial government had been permanently wrecked in the thirteenth century as a result of the emperor's commitments in Italy and the long struggle with the Papacy. The tendency toward the centralization of government operated there only within the smaller area of the territorial states which had been the great feudal fiefs of the medieval Empire. In the Low Countries, a group of counties and duchies, fiefs either of France or the Empire, were in the fourteenth and fifteenth centuries welded together to form a rich and strongly governed state under the Dukes of Burgundy. Spain did not exist as a national state until near the end of the fifteenth century, when Ferdinand of Aragon and Isabella of Castile united their states by marriage and expanded them by the conquest of Navarre and Granada. In central and northern Italy a unique situation had led to the decline of feudalism at an unusually early date. It had been replaced, however, not by strong central government but by a host of independent urban communes, turbulent little city-states, the wealthiest of which expanded by conquest to form territorial states of a quite unmedieval sort. We cannot here hope to trace the evolution of all the European states. I propose instead to concentrate attention on the two most distinct types: first, France and England, the feudal kingdoms which evolved into national monarchies, and, second, Milan, Venice, and Florence, the medieval communes which evolved into territorial states.

The process by which the kings of France and England recovered the governmental functions that had been parcelled out among the landholding lords and the self-governing communes operated especially in the four more or less distinct spheres of the administration of justice, military organization, economic regulation, and the collection of taxes. Of these the last was of the most all-pervasive importance.

Without some revenue the kings of the twelfth and thirteenth centuries could not have begun the task of expanding the scope of royal justice and of organizing an army on a national scale; but, having begun, they needed more and more revenue to meet the rising costs of government. In short, the more responsibilities the national governments assumed, the more revenue they had to have, and there seems to be a kind of iron law of fiscality according to which the financial needs of government always grow a step or two in advance of income. It is a problem not unfamiliar in our own age. The financial problems of the fourteenth and fifteenth century governments were also made even more acute than they otherwise might have been by the fact that the technique of warfare was changing in ways that made it increasingly expensive, a situation with which we are also not unfamiliar.

It was in the administration of justice that the kings first succeeded in making serious inroads upon the jurisdiction of the feudal lords. As the supreme feudal lord, the king could claim the right to hear appeals from the courts of his vassals and sub-vassals, and as the consecrated king he had not only the right but the duty to see that justice was done to all within his kingdom. The practical problem was to build up a royal government strong enough to enforce these claims, and this was a very gradual process, involving among other things the acquisition of increasing revenues. But the actual administration of justice placed no particular financial strain on the government, since the courts paid their way by levying fines and fees. In England, where the Norman conquest had introduced a more centralized form of feudalism than that prevailing on the continent, royal justice spread rapidly in the twelfth century. Under Henry II the system of sending out travelling justices from the king's court spread a uniform royal law, the common law of the land. At the end of the thirteenth century Edward I, the English Justinian, codified the common law in the form of statutes and virtually completed the absorption into the royal courts of all important criminal and civil cases. What remained of feudal jurisdiction was taken over in the following centuries by the justices of the peace, local gentry appointed by the crown, who served without pay but on the whole with admirable loyalty to the state.

In France, where feudalism was much more fully developed, that is, more decentralized, the triumph of royal justice was later and less complete. The French kings of the twelfth century had little jurisdiction beyond their own domain lands, a small area around Paris. During the following centuries, however, they expanded the domain to include one great fief after another and thus expanded the scope of their jurisdiction until it included the whole of the kingdom. But, even within the domain, feudal and seigneurial courts still existed and were never completely destroyed until the French Revolution. Nevertheless the king's justice spread steadily through his assertion of his right to hear appeals from the courts of his vassals and sub-vassals. In practice this process was carried out chiefly by a host of administrative officials, who were paid by receiving a portion of the fees and fines levied in the royal courts and so were eager to enlarge the business of these courts by extending royal jurisdiction as far as possible. These were the termites who gnawed away the foundations of feudal jurisdiction and carried on a ceaseless war of attrition against both seigneurial and communal courts. By the sixteenth century, in France as well as in England, one of the most essential functions of government had been recovered by the national state from the landholding lords who had usurped it in the early Middle Ages.

Along with the administration of justice and the maintenance of law and order, an equally important function of government is the defense of the state against the attacks of enemies from without or rebellion from within; and we can scarcely conceive of a state in which the central government does not assume full responsibility for the organization, equipment, and pay of the country's armed forces. Nor can we easily envisage a state in which all able-bodied citizens are not liable for military service. Yet in the early feudal state the king neither paid nor equipped an army, and he could do little to shape or control its organization. All he could do was call upon his vassals-in-chief to do the military service they owed—forty days or so a year—accompanied by such of their vassals as they could force to abandon their private feuds for a few weeks to serve the state. For all practical purposes, only the nobles were liable for military service, and they made up the only effective branch of the army, the heavy cavalry composed of armored knights. The majority of the population in the early feudal period consisted of serfs, who were not expected to fight. In a national emergency the king could call upon burghers and other freemen to serve as infantry, but these militia forces were poorly armed and poorly trained. Altogether, feudal armies were generally small, unreliable, undisciplined, and unmanageable on the field of battle. They were fit only for the local warfare that was the normal state of feudal society. For war on a national scale they were totally inadequate.

With increasing revenue, the kings of the twelfth and thirteenth centuries made some improvement in this situation by hiring foreign mercenaries and by paying a small permanent force, as well as by offering partial pay to vassals or commons who served beyond the customary time. The first decisive step toward the formation of a really national army did not, however, come until the last years of the thirteenth century, and then only in England. It was Edward I who reorganized the English army for his long campaigns in Wales and Scotland, and it was with this new type of royal army that his grandson, Edward III, later invaded France, where it demonstrated its decisive superiority over French armies that were still largely feudal in form and imbued with the undisciplined spirit of feudal chivalry.

Regular payment of wages on a graduated scale was an essential part of the new military organization. This made it

possible to hold the army together for long campaigns. It
also made possible the organization of the army into companies under royal officers who could impose discipline.
Without pay, too, it would have been difficult, if not impossible, for many knights to bear the rapidly rising cost of
armor in this period when heavy plate was beginning to re-
place the simpler chain mail of the crusading era. Fully
equipped knights were, of course, expensive, and the king of
a relatively poor country like England could not afford many
of them. Edward I probably had no more than 500 to 1000
knights for any of his campaigns, and his grandson's cavalry
force at Crécy probably consisted of no more than 1200
knights and perhaps twice as many mounted sergeants. What
made the English armies of this period so formidable was the
fact that the small but well equipped and trained cavalry
force was supported by a much larger force of equally well
trained and disciplined infantry, who were armed, moreover,
with the first really effective missile weapon known to the
Middle Ages, the deadly longbow. This weapon, the use of
which the English had learned the hard way from their
troublesome Welsh neighbors, was greatly superior to the
ancient short bow, which was all that Locksley's grandsire
could possibly have drawn at Hastings. It was also far superior in both range and rapidity of fire to the crossbow commonly used by continental archers. It had a range of
something up to 300 yards, and a skilled archer could loose
ten or twelve shafts a minute. It was, however, a weapon
that could be used effectively only after years of practice. It
would not have spread terror through France for more than
a hundred years had not the English archers been picked men,
carefully selected by royal officers from the growing class of
free yeomen farmers, who had made archery their national
sport and who, since the days of Edward I, had formed a
permanent militia reserve on which the king could draw at
will.

With all due respect to the longbow and the skill of the

English yeomen, however, there was a more fundamental reason for the consistent victories of the English army over much larger French forces during the greatest part of the Hundred Years' War. It was the balanced combination of cavalry and infantry tactics that destroyed the chivalry of France on the fields of Crécy and Poitiers. And tactics of any kind were possible only in a permanently organized and disciplined army. The Englishmen who fought from Crécy to Agincourt were professional soldiers who had taken the king's shilling and learned to obey commands. The French army, it is true, was also paid by the king and commanded by royal officers. The growing cost of armor, together with the general impoverishment of the nobility from economic and social causes too complex to discuss here, had made it necessary to pay even the king's noble vassals. The cost of warfare was, indeed, placing a crushing burden on the financial resources of the French government. But neither the French nobles nor the king could escape from the prejudices and traditional mores of feudalism sufficiently to adjust themselves to the new type of warfare. In the early days of the war the French army was not organized in uniform companies on a permanent basis. It was simply a paid feudal array, and the heavy cavalry was still regarded as the only important arm. At Crécy no use was made of the infantry, except for a few hundred mercenary Genoese crossbowmen, whom the French knights rode down when they got in the way. With no thought of tactics, and at Crécy against the express orders of the king, the French knights charged in massed formation again and again, only to be cut down in thousands by the hail of cloth-yard arrows from the English bowmen. In the years following Poitiers, Charles V abandoned the feudal levy and put the French army on something like a professional basis. He enrolled companies of native men-at-arms, as well as foreign mercenaries, and placed them under the command of Bertrand du Guesclin, a hardened old campaigner of relatively humble birth. It was not a very satisfactory system, for the mercenary companies were almost as destructive to French life and property as were the English enemy, but it was successful. While avoiding pitched battles, du Guesclin wore the invaders down by constant pressure, and when Charles V died in 1380, the English had lost everything they had gained in the early years of victory. In the long period of truce with England and civil war at home, which lasted through most of the reign of the mad king Charles VI, no further advance was made in the development of a national army. On the contrary, there was a kind of feudal revival, and when Henry V invaded France in 1415 the French commanders seemed to have forgotten the lessons of the previous century. Agincourt was a repetition of Crécy and Poitiers. The tide was finally turned against the English and the war brought to an end only after national sentiment had been rallied by the inspired patriotism of Joan of Arc, and Charles VII had organized a national army on a permanent basis, adequately paid and maintained by the state.

I have dealt at some length with the changes in military technique and organization because of the decisive part they played in shifting the balance of power within the state from the feudal nobility to the national monarchy. Let me underline some of the implications of this and add a point or two. Obviously, the substitution of a royal army for the more or less voluntary service of noble vassals was a triumph for the monarchy and a blow to both the prestige and the real power of the feudal lords. Obviously, too, the emergence of the infantry as an effective branch of the army was a blow to the nobles' monopoly of military force, on which their political power and independence had long rested securely. But there was more than this involved in the change. Infantry were effective only if well trained and well equipped and when used in fairly large bodies. That meant a permanent, paid force, which only a government supported by state taxation could afford. The introduction of firearms during the fifteenth century added further to the cost of maintaining infantry, and, incidentally, forced the knights to adopt heavier and heavier armor until it became a crushing burden in both the physical and financial sense. Finally, the development of artillery, chiefly as siege weapons, gave to state governments, which alone could afford such expensive pieces, the means by which to batter down the castles of rebellious nobles. Warfare, in short, was becoming a big business, too expensive to be indulged in as a private sport, as it had been during the feudal age. The wars of the sixteenth century were mostly international wars, fought by state governments, even when the motives might be religious or dynastic rather than national.

I need not, I think, labor further the point that as the central governments assumed more and more responsibilities they also required greatly increased revenues. The royal governments of this transitional period existed in a state of perpetual financial crisis. I cannot attempt to describe the various forms of taxation introduced in this period of fiscal experimentation by royal ministers who were prepared in their desperate need to try almost anything at least once. I would like, however, to point out briefly some of the ways in which the imposition of non-feudal taxes affected the evolution of national government.

In the first place, the central government could tax the great majority of the population only by going over the heads of the king's vassals to collect taxes directly from their dependents. This meant a vital infringement upon the private jurisdictions of the feudal lords, especially in France, where the royal government had less direct authority than in Norman England. It introduced the king's agents into every fief and *seigneurie*. And it established the direct contact between the king and the great mass of his subjects that was essential to the growth of a strong centralized state. So alien was state taxation to the ways of thinking of feudal society, however, that it could be introduced only as an extraordinary measure to meet some special emergency; and long after such emergencies had become normal annual occurrences, the subsidies the king demanded were still represented as extraordinary aids to the crown for the defense of the realm. For the same reasons, the kings in this transitional period found it advisable to negotiate with their subjects and to present their demands for taxes under the polite fiction that they were requests to which they asked the consent of clergy, nobles, and commons.

A second result of the king's growing need for taxes, then, was the development of representative institutions on a national scale: the English Parliament and the French Estates General. These institutions were an expansion of the king's feudal council by the addition of elected representatives of the non-noble bourgeoisie and, in England, of the landholding gentry also, who were empowered to give consent that would be binding upon the classes they represented. This, it is true, was not the only reason why the kings of the fourteenth century chose to summon representatives of the non-noble property-owning classes to their council. It was an important step in the process of establishing direct contact between the royal government and the people, or such of them at least as were economically, and therefore politically, important. But the problem of consent to taxation was always a primary consideration.

In France a fatal division of interest between the first two estates, the clergy and the nobles, both of which were composed largely of noble landowners, and the third estate, which represented the commercial bourgeoisie, prevented the Estates General from maintaining the advantage they had won in the fourteenth century. By the fifteenth century the French kings found it possible to levy direct taxes without consulting the estates, and thereafter ceased to summon them with any regularity. The estates, then, had simply enabled the monarchy to bridge the gulf between feudalism and absolutism. Having served the king's purpose, they ceased to exist. In England, on the other hand, where landholding gentlemen who shared the economic and social interests of the lords sat with representatives of the bourgeoisie in the House of Commons, Parliament was a more united and more genuinely representative body than the French Estates, and the kings were never able to ignore it with impunity. It would be sheer anachronism to think of Parliament in the first three centuries of its existence as a democratic body directing the affairs of the state. The most significant development of these centuries was the growth of the monarchy as an effective central government, which culminated in the semi-absolutism of the Tudors. Nevertheless, in the crowded chapter house at Westminster, seeds of representative government were planted that would eventually bear fruit throughout the English-speaking world.

One final by-product of the perpetual concern of royal government with the problem of revenue deserves mention, for it had an importance out of all proportion to the fiscal needs that inspired it. It was in these centuries that the central government gradually concentrated in its own hands the regulation of commerce and industry and shaped the national economic policy generally known as mercantilism. This development, too, had other causes than the king's need for taxes. It was, indeed, almost inevitable that as royal government grew stronger it would encroach upon the autonomy of the towns and cities which, in the feudal age, had been left almost entirely free to regulate their own economic life. Mercantilism was in many ways no more than the transference of the strict regulation of trade and the exclusive protectionism practiced by the medieval cities to the larger area of the state. Still, it was the fact that commerce and industry produced wealth in readily taxable form that first attracted the solicitous attention of money-hungry monarchs. Even when tariffs and other regulations were ostensibly designed to promote the general prosperity of the commonwealth, the royal government was primarily interested in the resulting revenue. Edward I and his successors would have been less interested in regulating and promoting the wool trade if the export tax on wool had not formed so large a part of the royal income—so large a part, indeed, that the Chancellor of the Exchequer took his seat in Parliament upon a woolsack, lest he forget for a moment on what foundation the royal treasury, which he personified, actually rested.

With the assumption of economic control by the central government, the triumph of the state over the local authorities that had dominated life in the Middle Ages was virtually complete. Thereafter the form of government might change, either by gradual evolution, as in England, or by revolution, as in most other European countries, but the state would remain the essential unit for the organization of modern society.

When we turn from the national states of the North to Italy, we find a very different situation; yet there too the Renaissance witnessed the development of a system of territorial states, though these were less than national in scope and they grew, not by the centralization of feudalism, but rather by the transformation and expansion of urban communes. The states of Renaissance Italy were necessarily different from those of the North, because the past history of Italy was so different, and that difference was partly the result of two purely political facts: first, the fact that from the tenth to the thirteenth century Italy was annexed to the German Holy Roman Empire and, second, that the popes ruled a territorial state stretching right across the center of the peninsula. Both emperor and pope claimed universal authority, and the inevitable conflict between them furnished the central theme of medieval Italian history, filling the land with sound and fury, but in the end signifying very little. The combined effect of the imperial *Anchluss* and the temporal sovereignty of the popes was to make the evolution of a national state in Italy impossible. That, however, is only half the story, and perhaps not the most important half. It was a purely economic fact—the extraordinary early and vigorous development of Italian commerce, a commerce built on the exchange of goods between the eastern Mediterranean and the lands of western Europe—that was responsible for the growth of rich and populous cities in the tenth and eleventh centuries. And it was the cities which, in the last analysis, were the decisive factor in the political life of central and northern Italy. They were the primary cause for the early decline of Italian feudalism, for as the cities grew in wealth and power the nobles were drawn into them as though by a golden magnet. And they were the real victors in the struggle between the Empire and the Papacy for, by playing off one against the other and exploiting the weaknesses of both, the cities were able to win for themselves a practically complete autonomy. When imperial power in Italy was permanently broken in the second half of the thirteenth century, and when the Papacy was transferred to Avignon at the beginning of the fourteenth century, the political void was filled by dozens of quarrelsome little city-states, each ruling the land around it and each pressing against its neighbors for more land to feed its people or for the control of essential trade routes.

Originally, these little city-states were self-governing communes with a republican form of government. This was a common medieval phenomenon. Except for the degree of their independence and the fact that they ruled the land around them, they were not very different in actual form of government from communes elsewhere in Europe. But just at the beginning of the Renaissance a vitally significant transformation was taking place in the majority of the communes, as republican government collapsed and was replaced by the rule of despots or, to use the less prejudiced Italian term, of *signori*. This change, which marks the first clear break between the medieval commune and the Renaissance state, is the outstanding fact in the political history of Italy in the fourteenth century, as many historians have recognized by calling this period the Age of the Despots. As we shall see presently, the foundation of the despots' power was not quite as illegitimate as Burckhardt and Symonds make it appear. Yet it is true that they ruled largely because they were able to do so, which argues a certain force of character and a considerable endowment of cunning, if not a high order of intelligence.

On the whole, the despots were colorful characters, patrons of the arts and much given to original sins, and they furnished inspiring material for those Romantic historians who like to think of the Renaissance as a wicked age, in which art and vice attained an equal degree of aesthetic refinement.

Once despotic government was established in a city, a new despot might take over by inheritance, conspiracy, conquest, or simply by purchasing it from the current incumbent. The question of prime interest to the historian, however, is why did republican government fail and how were the despots able, in the first place, to acquire dictatorial power? It is a question certainly not without interest in the twentieth century. A number of factors enter into this extremely complicated problem. The bitter animosity of the Guelf and Ghibelline parties inherited from the days when pope and emperor had partisans in every city, family feuds that grew into factional struggles, the danger of conquest by neighboring states, the action of strong personalities, all these contributed to the disintegration of the republics. But it seems to me that the fundamental factor was the division of the city population into distinct economic and social classes with divergent interests, which they were unwilling to sacrifice for the common good. As a rule, the *signori* first gained power in those cities in which the various classes were most evenly balanced, so that it proved impossible to maintain stable government, and the citizens, having lost faith in republican government and having grown weary of perpetual civil strife, permitted some strong man to assume control of the state.

This situation seems to have been particularly prevalent in the inland communes of Lombardy, of which Milan is the most famous example. Here a wealthy upper class had gained control of the city government in the period when the communes were struggling for independence. They had earned their right to power by bearing a large part of the cost of war and by serving as cavalry in the communal militia. This class was composed partly of old merchant families and partly of nobles who had moved into the city. By the thirteenth century they had mingled to form a purely urban aristocracy, which monopolized the government offices and dictated the city's policies. Meanwhile, as a result of the expansion of commerce and the growth of capitalist forms of business enterprise, new families were rising to wealth. There were thus two wealthy classes: the old and the new rich, the former clinging to political power and living more and more on inherited wealth and investments in land, the latter aggressively active in commerce and equally aggressive in demanding the share in political power to which their wealth entitled them. United, these two classes might have dominated the government securely. Divided, they opened the road to popular revolution, as the growing class of small shopkeepers and skilled artisans organized to fight for the political power that would enable them to protect their interests against the rich.

From this insoluble conflict of classes, complicated always by party and factional strife, the rule of one man emerged at first as a temporary measure. In one city after another the upper classes agreed to invite some distinguished foreigner to come in as a *podesta*, to take over the government for a one-year term and to impose peace on the troubled city. In many places, too, a popular revolution gave a similar temporary dictatorship to the leader of the popular party, the *capitano del popolo*, to whom the victorious *popolani* gave unlimited power so that he might wreak vengeance on their enemies. These offices were never intended to be held permanently, but once the citizens had surrendered the government to one man, it was difficult to recover it. The capacity for self-government tends to atrophy unless constantly exercised. Sooner or later, the offices of *podesta* or *capitano del popolo* would be extended to a longer term, then to a life tenure, and finally would become hereditary. At some point in this process the original title of office would be allowed to lapse and the dictator would be proclaimed *signore*, that is, lord of the city, and he would be invested with full and unlimited powers of government by the formal vote of the Great Council or some other body representing the citizens. How free such popular actions may have been we need scarcely question, nor does there seem much point in wondering what would have happened to any hardy citizen who voted against the *signore*. But the fact remains that he ruled by the consent, even if it was only the passive consent, of the people. Once established, the *signori*, scorning the base ascents by which they climbed, proceeded to obliterate as rapidly as possible all traces of the popular origin of their office. They secured a new legal sanction by purchasing the title of vicar from the emperor or the pope. Then, as the richer and more enterprising of them conquered other cities and built up a territorial state, they purchased the more resounding titles of marquis or duke from their territorial overlords. They were now princes, with all the semblance of legitimate sovereignty and the undisputed authority of absolute monarchs. Such were the Visconti and Sforza Dukes of Milan, the Estensi Dukes of Ferrara, and the Gonzaga Marquises of Mantua, and a score of petty princelings in the papal states.

So much for the question of why republican government failed in so many Italian communes. Despotism was the logical successor to a democracy that was not democratic and to a republic that had committed suicide. But the republics did not all collapse, nor did all Italians put their trust in princes. Our picture of the Italian states would be incomplete without some account of those republics that survived, especially Venice and Florence, the republics that grew into large territorial states.

Of all the Italian republics, Venice was the most stable, the most strongly organized, but also the least democratic. Venice was a commercial city in a sense that was scarcely true anywhere else. Having no land, it lived by commerce, and from the beginning its commerce was monopolized by a group of merchant families who formed the city's aristocracy. To protect their commercial monopoly, these patrician families established a watertight monopoly of political power and presented a united front against all demands by the mass of the populace for a voice in the government. In 1297, the Great Council was closed to all but the descendants of the families then in power. And, since the Venetian fleets were owned and controlled by the state, only members of the governing families were able to trade, so that no new families arose to threaten their power. Venice remained a republic, but a republic ruled by an oligarchy as arbitrary as any single despot.

The political history of Florence is much more complicated, partly because her economy was more complex and still in process of evolution in the thirteenth and fourteenth centuries, but partly also because the Florentine citizens seem to have combined with their unusual intellectual and aesthetic interests a passion for politics. At times, indeed, they demonstrated an ingenuity in the construction of involved political institutions that fell just short of lunacy.

Florence was a commercial city, but it was not a seaport, and its great economic expansion in the late thirteenth and early fourteenth centuries resulted from a combination of commerce with banking and large export industries, of which the woolen cloth industry was by far the most important and employed about a third of the city's ninety thousand population. This adventurous and many-sided capitalist economy afforded unusual opportunities for the creation of new fortunes, and as a result the composition of the class of wealthy merchant bankers and industrialists who generally succeeded in dominating the city's politics was constantly changing. New families rose to wealth, while old families went bankrupt or invested their inherited wealth in land and rents, or simply frittered it away. In the last years of the thirteenth century the new rich combined with the middle class of guildsmen to disenfranchise the old aristocracy and set up a government controlled by the merchant guilds, with a minor share allotted to the lesser guilds of shopkeepers and artisans. The great mass of

proletarian workers in the woolen industry, who were not permitted to organize in guilds, were excluded entirely from
active citizenship. One of the chief reasons why the merchant
employers in the great wool guilds felt it necessary to control
the government was to keep these restless workers in subjection. The middle class of small guildsmen also feared the violence of the woolworkers who crowded the slums of the city,
and so they generally followed the lead of the merchant industrialists. For a time in the middle of the fourteenth century, when the merchant class was weakened by depression
and a series of bank failures, the lesser guilds gained a larger
share in the government, but even then its policy was generally dictated by the merchant oligarchy.

The fact that executive power in the republican government was vested in a committee of priors, elected afresh every
two months, made it almost inevitable that some extra-con-
stitutional group should direct policy and give it some continuity. As a result, the vicissitudes of Florentine politics were
caused more by changes in the composition of the ruling clique
than in the republican constitution itself. When in 1434 a
group of new families headed by the banker Cosimo de
Medici took control from a clique of older families led by
the Albizzi, there was no revolutionary change in the constitution. To quote Schevill, "the new government was the old
government operated by a different set of beneficiaries."[7]
Under four generations of Medici leadership the republic
retained the semblance of democracy, although the sham
became increasingly apparent, while the Medici directed
affairs without holding actual public office, much after the
manner of a modern municipal boss. It was in foreign policy
especially, where continuity was absolutely essential, that the
Medici made themselves indispensable. They were not *signori*
in the ordinary sense of the word, but they took their place as
equals among the princes of Italy.

Foreign policy was becoming a matter of increasing im-

[7] F. Schevill, *History of Florence*, New York, 1936, p. 355.

portance to every Italian state in the fifteenth century, for by the beginning of that century the whole political structure of Italy had changed radically and was still changing. During the fourteenth century most of the petty despotisms of northern Italy had disappeared, swallowed up by the more powerful lordships of Padua, Verona, or Milan. At the end of the century nearly all of Lombardy, as well as a large part of Tuscany, had been drawn into the expanding state of Giangaleazzo Visconti, Duke of Milan. When he died in 1402 his personally acquired state broke up, but it had lasted long enough to alarm Venice by the fear that a large state in Lombardy might cut off her food supply and her trade routes to the Alpine passes. The merchant republic therefore embarked on a policy of landward expansion and proceeded to seize a large part of eastern Lombardy. Florence, too, took advantage of the temporary collapse of Visconti power to conquer all of Tuscany except Siena and Lucca. Nearly half a century of warfare finally ended with the Peace of Lodi in 1454, by which time all of Italy north of the papal states was divided between Venice, Milan, and Florence, with three or four small states maintaining a precarious existence between them. For the next forty years, until the arrival of the French invaders under Charles VIII, these states, together with the Papacy and the Kingdom of Naples, kept a fair degree of peace by carefully maintaining the balance of power. It is, I think, the first example of consciously calculated balance-of-power politics in the history of modern Europe.

In conclusion, I should like to say something about the interrelated problems of military force and revenue in the Italian states, as I did in relation to France and England, for herein is the secret of much of their strengths and their weaknesses. The Italian states of the Renaissance had no such difficulty with the introduction of a system of regular taxation as did the feudal kingdoms. The medieval communes had grown up with a money economy and the citizens were accustomed to taxation as a normal instrument of political life. The oli-

garchical republics like Venice and Florence merely rationalized and refined older customs. As for the despots, they
took over going concerns and had only to use reasonable dis-
cretion to operate them at a profit. The successful despot was
necessarily a good businessman, with a sharp eye on income,
for in the Renaissance states money was the indispensable
source of power. The citizens still paid taxes, but they no
longer served in the armed forces of the state, as they had
done in the heroic age of the communes. Instead, the states of
the fourteenth and fifteenth centuries depended for military
force entirely on hired mercenaries, homeless soldiers of fortune from every country in western Europe. The *condottieri*,
who commanded these mercenaries and sold their services to
the highest bidder, were essentially capitalist entrepreneurs.
They conducted war as a business, for a profit. They fought
only for pay, and the pay was high. From this situation two
things followed: first, that whoever controlled the treasury of
the state, whether despot or oligarchy, also controlled the
state's only armed force, before which the citizens were help-
less; and, second, that small and poor states could not com-
pete with larger and richer states which could hire more
soldiers. The conquest of the poorer states by the richer was
an inevitable result, as was demonstrated by the expansion of
Venice, Milan, and Florence. At the same time, any mercenary
army these states could afford was inadequate protection
against the national armies of France and Spain. The in-
vasion and subjection of Italy in the sixteenth century resulted
not only from the inability of the Italians to unite against the
foreigner, but also in large part from the fact that the Italian
people had long since left the business of warfare to mercenaries and had lost the art of self defense.

Though I have said little or nothing about the sixteenth
century, I feel this is justified by the relatively greater genetic
importance of the earlier and more formative period. The
most essential steps in the transition took place during the
fourteenth and fifteenth centuries. The sixteenth century

simply completed the process, consolidated the authority already won by the central governments, established a state system in western Europe based on the balance of power, and raised to a more conscious level the national sentiment bred in the conflicts of the preceding centuries. The feudal concept of the state as a complex of personal relations finally gave way in the North, as it had already done in Italy, to the concept of the state as a single political entity. In the sixteenth century, when every prince read Machiavelli or acted as though he had done so, when international wars and diplomacy held the center of the European stage, and when all men looked more and more to the government of the state for the regulation of their economic and social life, in that century the modern state came of age. This was the century in which national literatures finally triumphed over the Latin culture common to all Christendom. Even religion assumed a national character and fell to a certain extent under the control of the state. The Protestant Reformation destroyed the unity of the Christian faith and replaced it with national churches organized under the authority of the state. Where the old church survived it was forced to compromise and to share its authority with the state. In the sixteenth century feudal particularism and the universal Christian commonwealth both disappeared, leaving in their place the national state to form the matrix in which modern civilization would be cast.

II HARD TIMES AND
INVESTMENT IN CULTURE

by Robert S. Lopez

When humanists like Michelet and Burckhardt accredited the term Renaissance, a good many years ago, economic history had hardly been born. Their lofty reconstruction of civilization in the Renaissance was unencumbered by the suspicion that the passions of Caliban might have had something to do with the achievements of Ariel. Then came the followers of Marx and historical materialism, who trimmed the wings of the poet-historians and inserted literature into the digestive process. We ought to pay our deepest respects to both schools, not only to set an example to posterity when our own turn in obsolescence comes, but also because both the brain and the stomach certainly have an influence on the movements of the heart.

Historians, however, after letting the pendulum swing fully in either direction, have labored to find an equilibrium and a chain of relations between cause and effect. The easiest way to link two unfolding developments is to describe them as parallel and interlocked at every step. The notion that wherever there was an economic peak we must also find an intellectual peak, and vice versa, has long enjoyed the unquestioned authority of mathematical postulates. In an examination book of a sophomore which I graded not so long ago, the postulate entailed these deductions: Double-entry bookkeeping in the Medici Bank goaded Michelangelo to conceive and accomplish the Medici Chapel; contemplation of the Medici Chapel in turn spurred the bankers to a more muscular management of credit. But these statements, even if they were more skilfully worded, are quite misleading. There is no denying that many beautiful homes of the Renaissance belonged to successful businessmen—in Italy above all, then in Flanders, in southern Germany, and in other regions. Yet if bankers like the Medici and the Fuggers had been capable of conjuring up artists like Michelangelo and Dürer, then our own Rothschilds and Morgans ought to have produced bigger and better Michelangelos. And how could we explain the emergence of Goya in an impoverished Spain, or the artistic obscurity of the business metropolis that was Genoa? A minimum of subsistence is indispensable for art and a minimum of intelligence is indispensable for business. But this does not mean that great artists and great businessmen must be born in the same group and in the same generation.

What strikes us at the outset is the different relation between economy and culture in the high Middle Ages and in the Renaissance. I must beg leave to begin by a very brief description of what we call the "commercial revolution" of the high Middle Ages. This great economic upheaval, comparable in size only to the modern industrial revolution, surged from the Dark Ages at about the same time as the *chansons de geste* and early Romanesque art. It reached its climax in the age of Dante and rayonnant Gothic, after which a great depression occurred. Like the modern industrial revolution, it was a period of great, continuous demographic growth, of steady if not spectacular technological progress, of expansion both through increased production and consumption at home and through conquest of new markets abroad. It was an epoch of great opportunities and great hopes, of small wars for limited objectives, and of growing toleration and interchange of ideas among persons of different classes, nations, and beliefs. Its pace was, of course, slower than that of the industrial revolution, because progress traveled by horse and galley rather than by train, steamship, and airplane. The final results, however, were probably of the same order of magnitude. The medieval commercial revolution was instrumental in bringing about the momentous changes which bequeathed to the Renaissance a society not too different from our own, and was in turn influenced by all of these changes. It caused the old feudal system to crumble and the old religious structure to weaken. It all but wiped out slavery; it gave liberty to serfs over large areas, and created a new elite based upon wealth rather than birth.

A great expansion in all other fields occurred at the same time. The blossoming of a new literature and art, the revival of science and law, the beginning of political and religious individualism, the spread of education and of social consciousness to larger strata of the population, were concurrent and contemporaneous with the commercial revolution of the high Middle Ages. Though not all facets of medieval literature and philosophy were such as one might expect of an age of economic expansion, who will deny that there was a connection between economic and intellectual progress? It is also proper to suggest that the economic and social change of the high Middle Ages was an indispensable preparation for the Renaissance, even as it is safe to state that a man must have been an adolescent before he can become a father. But we must not confuse two different ages. Probably there would have been no Renaissance—or, rather, the Renaissance would have taken another course—if the Middle Ages had not previously built the towns, humbled the knights, challenged the clergymen, and taught Latin grammar. But the towns of the Middle Ages created the civilization of the Middle Ages. Whether or not this civilization was as great as that of the Renaissance, it certainly was different.

Let us not say that the general coincidence of an exuberant civilization and an expansive economy in the high Middle Ages shows that great art and great business must always go together. Consider the different experience of different countries. Italy was to the medieval economic process what England was to that of the eighteenth and nineteenth centuries. It was the cradle and the pathfinder of the commercial revolution, which was on the move in several Italian towns long before it made its way through the rest of Europe. Like the industrial revolution, the commercial revolution did not spread evenly: here it passed by large areas or slackened its speed, there it gained impetus as it engulfed other generators of economic advance. In Flanders, for instance, the currents coming from Italy swelled a river which had sprung from local streams. But Ile de France, the home of so much glorious medieval art, literature, and philosophy, was a retarded if not quite a forgotten area. Its towns were small and sleepy in the shadow of the great cathedrals at a time when the Italian towns hummed with business activity and made great strides in the practical sciences of law, mathematics, and medicine, but had not yet produced a Dante, a Giotto, or an Aquinas.

With these three giants Italy concluded the Middle Ages in a thoroughly medieval way. Petrarch, another Italian, ushered in the intellectual Renaissance at the very moment when the economic trend was reversed. The exact span of the Renaissance is variously measured by historians of civilization. There was a time lag between the Renaissance in Italy and that of the other countries. Moreover, the imperialism of certain lovers of the Renaissance has led them to claim as forerunners or followers men who would be better left to the Middle Ages or to the Baroque. I shall assume that, chronologically speaking, the Renaissance means roughly the period between 1330 and 1530, though the economic picture would not substantially change if we added a few decades at the beginning or at the end. Now that period was not one of economic expansion. It was one of great depression followed by a moderate and incomplete recovery.

Time alone will tell whether the economy of the age in which we live is the early stage of another "Renaissance" rather than the prelude to another "Dark Age," or a mere pause before another cycle of expansion. We shall see in a moment that certain resemblances seem to bring the Renaissance closer to us than any other historical period, in the economic field as in many others. But there was no resemblance in regard to population trends. Following a great plunge in the mid-fourteenth century, the population of Europe tended to stagnate at a far lower level than that of the high Middle Ages. A number of epidemics, far more terrible than any medieval contagion, whittled down the population. Famines, birth control, and other causes which cannot be enumerated here even in the most summary fashion, contributed to the same end. The decline was particularly pronounced in cities—the very homes of the essentially urban civilization that was the Renaissance. The country suffered less and recovered better, but it did not escape the general pattern.

The falling curve of the population was to some extent connected with other retarding factors. Technological progress continued but, with the notable exceptions of the insurance contract, the printing press and certain advances in metallurgy, it was represented by diffusion and improvement of medieval methods and tools rather than by the invention of new ones. True, there was Leonardo da Vinci; but his amazing inventions were of no avail to his contemporaries, who were uninformed of and probably uninterested in them. Again, the Renaissance introduced a better type of humanistic school and superior education for the elite, but it made no sweeping changes in technical education and no significant advances in bringing literacy to the masses. In these respects the Renaissance was less "modern" than the high Middle Ages.

A closer resemblance to our own times lies in the fact that the gradual shrinking of political horizons frustrated the improved means of transportation and the powerful organization of international trade which the Middle Ages had bequeathed to the Renaissance. Shortly before the Renaissance began, a Florentine merchant had described the road from the Crimea to Peking as perfectly safe to westerners—a statement which we would hesitate to make today. But, during the Renaissance, East and West were split deeply, first by the collapse of the Mongolian Empire in the Far and Middle East, then by the Turkish conquest in the Near East. A medieval

advance in the opposite direction was nullified before its possibilities were grasped: the Scandinavians abandoned Vinland,
Greenland, and Iceland. Within Europe each state manifested
its incipient centralization by raising economic barriers against
all of the others. To be sure, the twilight of the Renaissance
was lighted up by the greatest geographic discoveries. But it
was a long time before the beneficial effects of the new round
of discoveries were felt. The first telling result was the dis-
ruptive revolution of prices through the flood of American
silver and gold—and even this came when the Renaissance
had already been seized by its gravediggers, the Reformation and the Counter-Reformation.

War and inflation were as familiar to the Renaissance as
they are, unfortunately, to us. It is true that already in the
high Middle Ages a continuous but gradual and moderate inflation of the coinage and a parallel growth of credit money
had provided much needed fuel for the demographic and
economic expansion of the commercial revolution. But in the
Renaissance inflation was steeper and steeper. Soft money
did not supply larger means of payment for a growing number of producers and consumers. It was chiefly turned out by
monarchies and city-states to pay for the largest wars that
had afflicted Europe since the fall of the Roman world—the
largest that Europe was to witness before the Napoleonic
period, or perhaps our own world wars. One thinks first of the
Hundred Years War, which, with some intermediate truces,
lasted well over a century and plagued most of western
Europe. The Angevin-Aragonese contest was smaller in scope,
but it desolated the whole of southern Italy and Sicily for
almost two hundred years. The Turkish armies inflicted still
greater sufferings upon southeastern and east-central Europe.
In northern Italy the mercenaries may have been gentle when
fighting one another, but they were a plague to private har-
vests and public treasuries. Germany was the theatre of inces-
sant local wars and brigandage, and Spain was hardly more
peaceful. It is true that in the second half of the fifteenth cen-

tury most of Europe had some respite. But then came the wars between the Hapsburgs and France, with intervention by the Turks, which involved the whole of Europe, used artillery on a large scale, and renewed atrocities that had almost disappeared in the high Middle Ages. They had not ended when the wars of religion began.

Needless to say, disease and famine were faithful companions of war. Moreover, during the fourteenth century desperate revolts of peasants and city proletarians burst out almost everywhere from England to the Balkans and from Tuscany to Flanders. They also claimed their victims. In the fifteenth century a dull resignation seemed to prevail, and banditism sprouted, sometimes even in the vicinity of towns. The early sixteenth century was marred by terrible peasants' revolts in Hungary, Germany, northeastern Italy, Switzerland, and northern France.

Then, as now, inflation was not enough to support the burden of war. Taxation rose to much higher levels than during the commercial revolution, when a booming economy could have borne it more easily. It fleeced peasants and landlords, but it skinned the bourgeoisie, which had greater amounts of cash. In France and England the Renaissance marked the downfall of town autonomy, largely though not exclusively because the towns were unable to balance their budgets and because the richer bourgeoisie, who could have come to the assistance of their poorer fellow-citizens, refused to bear even their own full share. In Italy the independent towns survived, at a price. They fell under dictators, who brought about some equalization of burdens through universal oppression; or under small oligarchies of very rich men, who could either bear or evade taxation.

Yet it would not be fair to ascribe to taxation alone the principal blame for an economic recession which was essentially caused by shrinking or dull markets. The markets had shrunk because the population had diminished or stagnated, and because the frontier had receded and had been locked up.

Perhaps some compensation would have been found through a better distribution of wealth if the scattered revolts of the fourteenth century had grown into a general social revolution. They failed. The recurrence of wars and epidemics throttled whatever social ferment remained in the fifteenth century. In the general stagnation some of the rich men grew richer, many of the poor men grew poorer, and the others at best obtained security at the expense of opportunity.

The ominous signs are visible everywhere. Land prices and landlords' profits in the Renaissance were at their lowest ebb in centuries. The great movement of land reclamation and colonization which had characterized the centuries between the tenth and the early fourteenth was arrested. As early as the thirteenth century, to be sure, many landlords in England, in Spain, in southern Italy, and in northwestern France had transformed arable land into sheep ranges. Wool was a good cash crop and sheep farming required little manpower. The process continued throughout the Renaissance, but it became less and less rewarding as the demand for wool became stagnant or declined. Great patches of marginal and even fairly good land, which had been exploited in the Middle Ages, were now returned to waste. Fertile estates were sold or rented for nominal prices. But even these low prices were too high for many hungry, landless peasants who lacked even the small capital needed to buy seeds and tools. Fortunate was the peasant whose lord was willing to advance money in return for a share of the crop.

In the high Middle Ages the towns had absorbed not only an ever increasing amount of foodstuffs and industrial raw materials, but also the surplus product of the human plant. Noblemen, yeomen, and serfs, each one according to his capacity, could then easily find occupation and advancement in town. In the Renaissance, opportunities were usually reserved for those who were citizens of the town. Yet citizens, too, had little chance to improve their lot. The guilds formerly had accepted apprentices freely and assured every apprentice of the opportunity of becoming a master. Now they became rigid hierarchies; only the son of a master could hope to succeed to the mastership. Outsiders were either rejected or kept permanently in the subordinate position of journeymen. This trend also affected the guilds of artists. Occasionally, to be sure, a town encouraged immigration of qualified groups of countrymen on condition that they carry out the humbler industrial tasks at lower salaries than those of the lowest journeymen. Again, the old practice of putting out raw materials for peasants to work at home gained some ground, but the increase of manufacturing in the country fell far short of compensating for the decrease of industrial production in towns. It was not a symptom of economic growth but merely a means of depressing wages. Luxury industries alone maintained and perhaps increased their production. This reflects the decline of production for the masses and the growing distance between the very rich and the very poor.

The growing dullness of European markets and the loss of many eastern markets was bound to depress commerce. The leitmotif now was to offer for sale, not the greatest quantity and variety of goods, but, to quote a fifteenth-century manual of business "only as much as one can sell in the place of destination." Nor was it always possible to buy as much as one desired. Wars and embargoes frequently interfered with trade. Increased duties in nearly every country from England to Egypt raised the cost of many wares to prohibitive heights. The age of rapid fortunes won in daring oversea and overland ventures was over. Sedentary merchants could still maintain their position if they employed many able and loyal employees and commission agents, if they planned every step carefully, and if they could wait patiently for their investments to bring hard-won profits. In Italy five to eight per cent was now regarded as a fair interest rate in commercial loans—a much lower rate than those prevailing in the high Middle Ages, although risks had not diminished. Banks improved their methods and often increased their size while diminishing in numbers. But they had to use a larger and larger proportion of their capital not for trade but for loans to the idle upper class and more frequently to belligerent states. Such investments usually brought high interest for a very short period and failure when the debtor was unable to pay the principal.

One business, insurance, boomed during the Renaissance. It bordered on gambling. Investors had no statistics to rely upon. Risky speculations on foreign exchange also drained capital away from commercial investments. Overt gambling attracted ambitious men who despaired of other gainful occupations. There were the extreme cases of scoundrels who staked their money against the life of an unknowing person and had that person murdered so that they could cash the bet. At the other extremity were many business men who abandoned trade and invested in land, not merely a part of their capital, as merchants had always done, but everything they had. Even when bought at the lowest prices, land was not very remunerative; but it could insure some reward for the owner who sank enough money in improvements and administered the investment in the spirit of business. The shift of production from butter to guns was reflected in the different fortune of merchants who exploited mines. After a long slump in mining there was a sudden boom in the late fifteenth and early sixteenth centuries. Metallurgy prospered: iron and bronze were raw materials, and precious metals were the sinews of war. They also were needed to pay tributes to the Turks and increased custom duties to the Egyptians. But alum, a basic material for the declining cloth industry, was not in great demand. When the mines increased their output, the price of alum fell.

Italy, the earliest and most brilliant center of the artistic Renaissance, felt the impact of the economic recession most heavily. Its condition resembled somewhat that of England after 1918, or that of New England after 1929. Italy fell harder because it had climbed higher. It had exploited most of its possibilities, and it could not seek recovery by opening up many new fields of enterprise. Conversely, those countries which watered down their intellectual Renaissance with the largest proportion of medieval strains also seem to have felt the shock of the economic crisis less deeply.

Of course, we must not overstress the dark side of the picture. Contraction and stagnation had succeeded expansion, but the economic ceiling of the fifteenth century was still much higher than the top level of the twelfth, though it was lower than the peak of the thirteenth. The bourgeoisie preserved its commanding position in Italy and its influence in the western monarchies. The amazing progress of the commercial revolution in methods and techniques was not lost; indeed, the depression spurred businessmen to further rationalization and sounder management. Thanks to their accumulated experience and capital, the Italians not only defended their leading position but also quickened the recovery of other countries by investing capital and frequently establishing their residence abroad. Some countries which had formerly been retarded felt the full impact of the commercial revolution only now.

Finally, the depression and even the greatest disasters were sources of profit for some men. In many places food prices declined faster than real wages. Cheap land and cheap manpower made the fortune of many entrepreneurs. War enabled Jacques Coeur to grab fabulous riches. Inflation was a boon to the Fuggers, who controlled silver and copper mines. Southern Germany gained from the disruption of communications through France and, later, from the ruin of Venetian and Florentine banks. Barcelona inherited some of the trade which had slipped from Pisa. Antwerp fell heir to the commerce, though not to the industry, of other Flemish towns. Some of these successes were fleeting. Others lasted as long as the Renaissance. None of them, however, was as durable as had been the commercial and industrial blossoming of Italy and Belgium or the prime of English and French agriculture in the high Middle Ages. Qualitatively and quantitatively the compensations fell short of the deficiencies.

Economic historians are usually expected to back their statements with figures. These are not easily tested for a period which had not yet learned how to use statistics for the information of friends and the misinformation of enemies. Still, what statistical data we have are reliable enough as indications of trends in growth or decrease, if not as absolute indexes of size. Here are some figures:

In 1348 the population of England was at least 3,700,000. In the early fifteenth century it plunged as low as 2,100,000. Then it rose slowly, but as late as 1545 it was still half a million short of the pre-Renaissance level. Yet England suffered comparatively little from war, and presumably was less affected by the economic slump than were some more advanced countries. Again, Florence in the time of Dante had more than 100,00 inhabitants, but no more than 70,000 in the time of Boccaccio, and approximately the same number in the time of Michelangelo. Zürich, a typical middle-size town, fell from 12,375 inhabitants in 1350 to 4,713 in 1468. Similar declines can be measured for the larger part of towns and countries. As for the often cited compensating factors, Antwerp, the one Belgian town whose population increased in the Renaissance while that of all the others decreased, in 1526 had 8,400 houses. There still were as many houses in Bruges, its ruined rival. Again, Catalonia, one of the few countries which continued to grow after the early fourteenth century, rose from 87,000 to 95,000 homesteads from 1359 to 1365. But it declined to 59,000 in 1497, and it was still down at 75,000 in 1553.

To turn to another kind of figures, the incoming and outgoing wares subject to tax in the port of Genoa were valued at £3,822,000 Genoese in 1293. The figure fell to £887,000 in 1424. In 1530 it was still more than one million short of the 1293 level, in spite of the fact that the purchasing power of the pound had greatly declined in the interval. Again, the aggregate capital of the main house and seven of the eight branches of the Medici bank in 1458 was less than 30,000 florins, whereas the capital of the Peruzzi bank in the early fourteenth century had risen above the 100,000 florin mark. Yet the Medici company in the Renaissance towered above all other Florentine companies, whereas the medieval Peruzzi company was second to that of the Bardi. Similarly, the combined fortunes of the three richest members of the Medici family in 1460 were valued at only fifteen per cent more than the fortune of one Alberti merchant a hundred years earlier. As for the so-called compensating factors, it is true that in 1521 Jakob Fugger the Rich obtained from Emperor Charles V an acknowledgment of debt for 600,000 florins. But in the early fourteenth century the English king owed the Bardi company an equal sum, according to English documents, which probably underestimated the debt, or 900,000 florins according to Villani, who may have overestimated it. In addition, the English king owed the Peruzzi company a sum two thirds as large.

The woolen industry affords the best examples in regard to manufacturing because it worked chiefly for an international market. Without leaving Florence, we note that in 1378 the weavers went on strike to demand of the industrialists that they should pledge a minimum yearly output of 24,000 pieces of cloth. Forty years earlier the yearly output had been between 70,000 and 80,000 pieces. Yet the depression did not hit Florence as hard as Flanders, her greater rival. The slow growth of English woolen industry, which occurred at the same period, was far from compensating the decline of production in the other major centers. Total export figures very seldom exceeded 50,000 pieces, and usually were not higher than 30,000.

It is harder to put one's finger upon agrarian figures. But we may regard as suitable examples the contraction of cultivated areas and the falling prices of agricultural products in a time of general monetary inflation. In Prussia the price of rye fell by almost two thirds between 1399 and 1508. In England the price of grain declined by forty-seven per cent between 1351 and 1500, and that of cattle and animal products declined by thirty-two per cent. "Of the 450 odd [English] manors for which the fifteenth-century accounts have been studied, over 400 show a contraction of land in the hands of tenants." In Gascony after 1453 "thirty per cent of the rural villages were ravaged or seriously damaged." The plain of southern Tuscany, which had been reclaimed in the high Middle Ages, now relapsed to its previous condition of a malaria-ridden waste. In Castile the most powerful company of sheep owners in 1477 owned 2,700,000 sheep, or roughly a sheep for every other inhabitant of the country. Figures of this kind, and the frequent reports about starvation and vagrancy, more than offset what information we have on agricultural progress in some parts of Lombardy and the introduction of some new plants to France.

I hope all this is enough to show that the Renaissance was neither an economic golden age nor a smooth transition from moderate medieval well-being to modern prosperity. I have fired only a small part of the available ammunition; still less would have been needed but for the fact that the newer findings of economic historians do not easily pierce the crust of preconceived impressions. Is it necessary to add that nobody should jump to the opposite conclusion and contend that the coincidence of economic depression and artistic splendor in the Renaissance proves that art is born of economic decadence? I do not think it is. We have just seen that the peak of medieval economy coincided with the zenith of medieval art.

A more insidious path would be open to straight economic determinism if someone invoked the overwrought theory of cultural lags. Cultural lags, as everybody knows, are ingenious, elastic devices to link together events which cannot be linked by any other means. Someone might suggest that a cultural lag bridged the gap between the economic high point of the thirteenth century and the intellectual high point of the fifteenth, so that the intellectual revolution of the Renaissance was a belated child of the commercial revolution of the Middle Ages. What should one answer? Personally, I doubt the paternity of children who were born two hundred years after the death of their fathers. To be sure, the Renaissance utilized for its development the towns which the Middle Ages had built, the philosophy which the Greeks had elaborated, and nearly everything else that mankind had contrived ever since Neanderthal; but its way of life was conditioned by its own economy and not by the economy of the past.

There is no heap of riches and no depth of poverty that will automatically insure or forbid artistic achievement. Intellectual developments must be traced primarily to intellectual roots. But that does not at all mean that they are independent of economic conditions. The connection is not a direct and crude relation of cause and effect. It is a complicated harmony in which innumerable economic factors and innumerable cultural factors form together a still greater number of chords. That some of them are incongruous or dissonant should not surprise us. Every age is full of contradictions.

We have a unison rather than an accord when the literature and the art of the Renaissance make direct allusions to the troubled economic cricumstances. Machiavelli in his *History of Florence* is well aware of the crisis, its causes and its manifestations. Martin Luther inveighs against the consequences of economic causes which he does not clearly perceive. The anonymous author of *Lazarillo de Tormes* embraces in his sympathetic irony the disinherited of all social classes. Agrippa d'Aubigné decribes in Biblical terms the terrible sufferings of France. Donatello and Jerome Bosch crowd their bas-reliefs and their paintings with portraits of starved persons. The enumeration could continue, but it would bring little light to the interrelation of economics and culture. What we look for is not the direct image of economic facts, but the indirect repercussions of these facts on the development of ideas.

Of the many connections that might be suggested, some

are too farfetched and dubious for an earthly economic historian to take stock of them. For instance, some clever contrivance might be found to link together economic rationalization and intellectual rationalism. One might compare the clarity and symmetry of Renaissance double-entry books of accounting to the clarity and symmetry of Renaissance buildings. But the Renaissance also created such poems as that of Ariosto, which is anything but symmetrical, and such philosophies as that of Marsilio Ficino, which is anything but clear. Moreover, double-entry accounting was not a monopoly of the Renaissance. It made its first appearance in the early fourteenth century, if not earlier, and it is still used today. Perhaps we should leave these lofty comparisons to the examination book which I cited at the beginning.

More definite connections probably existed between specific economic factors and some themes or fashions in the literature, art, and thought of the Renaissance. Consider, for instance, the theme of the Wheel of Fortune, which is one of the refrains of the age. To be sure, the blind goddess at all times has exercised her influence upon all forms of human activity. But her way has seldom been as capricious and decisive as in the Renaissance, when gambling was one of the principal means of making a fortune, and when ill fortune alone could unseat the fortunate few who were sitting pretty. Then consider the vogue of pastoral romance and the fresh interest in country life. The country always has its fans and its idealizers. Still, its charm must have been particularly alluring to merchants who returned to the country after generations of rush to the city. They found there not only a better investment but also a healthier atmosphere and a more sincere way of life. Again, the list could easily be lengthened, but it might seem an anti-climax to those who are waiting for a comprehensive interpretation of the interplay of economy as a whole and culture as a whole. I shall not attempt to concoct a catch-all formula, which would only conceal the endless variety of actions and reactions. No harm is done, however, if the discordant details are grouped in tentative generalizations.

We have seen that the essential phases of Renaissance economy were first a depression, then stabilization at a lower level than the highest medieval summit. The implicit opposition between those two trends, depression and stabilization, may perhaps help us to understand a certain dualism in the general outlook of the Renaissance. Note that I said "may help to explain," not "explain." I am not postulating direct causes, but what my brilliant colleague, Mr. Ferguson, would call "permissive or partially effective causes." Some Renaissance men were pessimists: they thought of the lost heights rather than of the attained platform. Others, especially those who had managed to settle down in sufficient comfort, felt that they had definitely and finally arrived.

The pessimists may not have been the larger group, but they seem to have included some of the most significant personalities, ranging from Savonarola to Machiavelli, from Leonard da Vinci to Michelangelo, from Dürer to Cervantes, from Thomas More perhaps to William Shakespeare. It would be useless to list more names without accounting for their inclusion, but I may be allowed, as an economic historian, to point out some of the intellectual aspects of depression. Some pessimists joined the medieval preachers in demanding an earnest return to God, or they imitated the pagan writers in exalting the golden age of primitive mankind. Others maintained that all human history, or indeed the history of the universe, is a succession of cycles in growth and decay, with no hope for permanent progress. Still others built political theories upon the assumption that men are basically gullible and corrupt, and that a statesman must adapt his strategy to human imperfection. Similar assumptions underlay many tragedies, comedies, and novels. Quite a few pessimists voiced the plight of the poor and the weak, or portrayed them in the background—but seldom in the forefront, because the forefront was reserved for the rich and the strong who purchased the work of art. A number invoked death or sleep, the brother of death. A larger number sought an escape from reality, not in Heaven but in a world of artistic, literary, philosophical, or even mathematical dreams. All of these diverse trends may of course be detected during any historical period, but they seem more pronounced during the Renaissance. It is easier to link them with economic depression than with any other economic trend.

The optimists in the Renaissance were not as different from the pessimists as one might think at first. Usually they shared with the pessimists a widespread belief in the flow and ebb of civilization, and a tendency to look for an ideal of perfection in the past and not in the future. Their standard, however, was nothing like the coarse emotionalism of the Middle Ages or the naive primitiveness of the mythical Golden Age. It was classic antiquity—another age of stability and poise in aristocratic refinement. The optimists thought that antiquity had been one of the high tides in human history, and that their own time was another high tide, intimately close to antiquity and utterly unrelated to the recent past. Now was the time to stretch one's hand for the riches which the high tide brought within reach. One could be Horatian and pluck the rose of youth and love before her beauty had faded. One could be more ambitious and make every effort to comprehend, fulfil, and enjoy the greater wealth which was now accessible to men freed from instinct and ignorance. Private individuals and political leaders were equally impatient. Their drive for self-fulfilment was humanitarian and peaceful so long as they strove to discover and develop their own selves, their own moral and material resources. But it had to become aggressive individualism and political ruthlessness when success depended upon conquest of resources claimed by other individuals or nations. All of these characteristics, too, can be found in other ages, but they seem to predominate in the Renaissance. They are not surprising in an economic stagnation which still offers a good life to the elite but little hope for the outcast.

The moods of the Renaissance are so many and so various that they seem almost to defy definition. That is exactly why the Renaissance looks so modern to us—it was almost as rich and diversified as the contemporary scene. One important modern trait, however, was lacking. Most of its exponents had little faith and little interest in progress for the whole human race. Indeed this idea seems to be germane to economic expansion. The religious ideal of progress of mankind from the City of Man towards the City of God hardly survived the end of the commercial revolution and the failure of social revolts in the fourteenth century. In the later period, even the most pious men tended to exclude forever from the City of God the infidel, the heretic, and frequently all but a handful of Catholic ascetics or Protestant militant men predestined for salvation. The secular ideal of the progress of mankind through the diffusion of decency and learning was seldom emphasized before the late sixteenth century, when economic stagnation began at last to be broken. In between there were nearly two hundred years—the core of the Renaissance—during which any hope for progress was generally held out not to the vulgar masses but to individual members of a small elite, not to the unredeemable "barbarians" but to the best representatives of chosen peoples.

Contrary to widespread popular belief, the society of the Renaissance was essentially aristocratic. It offered economic, intellectual, and political opportunities to only a small number. But it lacked a universally accepted standard of nobility. The commercial revolution of the high Middle Ages and the social changes connected with it already had undermined the aristocracy of blood. The great depresssion of the mid-fourteenth century, and the stagnation which followed shook the security and whittled down the income of the aristocracy of wealth. Blood and money, of course, were still very useful (they always are) but neither insured durable distinction by itself. Too many landowners, merchants, and bankers had lost or were threatened with losing their wealth, and high birth without wealth was of little avail in the age which has been called "the heyday of illegitimate children." Neither was there any recognized hierarchy of states and nations. The Holy Roman Empire of the Germanic people had fallen to pieces; the Papacy had come close to total dissolution; France and England rose and fell many times; the Italian city-states witnesed a stunning series of *coups d'etat* and mutations of fortune.

Perhaps this was why culture, what we still call humanistic culture, tended to become the highest symbol of nobility, the magic password which admitted a man or a nation to the elite group. Its value rose at the very moment that the value of land fell. Its returns mounted when commercial interests rates declined. Statesmen who had tried to build up their power and prestige by enlarging their estates now vied with one another to gather works of art. Business men who had been looking for the most profitable or the most conservative investments in trade now invested in books. The shift was more pronounced in Italy because in Italy businessmen and statesmen were the same persons. And it is in this field, I believe, that we can most profitably investigate the relation between economic and intellectual trends of the Renaissance. We ought to explore briefly the increased value of humanistic culture as an economic investment.

Quite probably the increase was relative and not absolute. It is doubtful that the Renaissance invested in humanistic culture more than any period of the Middle Ages. The precious metals which early medieval artists lavished in their works were a staggering proportion of the available stocks of gold and silver. The cathedrals and castles of the twelfth century probably absorbed a greater amount of raw materials and manpower-hours than the churches and palaces of the Renaissance. Medieval universities were far greater investments, in strictly economic terms, than the humanistic schools. But universities, cathedrals and castles were not built primarily—or, at least, not exclusively—for the sake of pure humanistic culture. Universities aimed at preparing men for professional careers, such as those of clergyman, lawyer, and physician. Castles were insurances against accidents in this life. It is not surprising that shrewd rulers and thrifty business men were prepared to invest part of their capital in functional works of art and in practical culture.

The investment, however, often was inversely proportional to the intensity of business spirit. We have noted that northern France, the home of most of the largest cathedrals, was one of the retarded countries in the commercial revolution. Let us now point out that cathedrals in northern Italy and Tuscany were usually smaller than those of France. Paris had the largest faculty of theology, whereas Italian universities stressed the more practical studies of law and medicine. Genoa, perhaps the most businesslike town in medieval Italy, had one of the smallest cathedrals and no university at all. Yet its inhabitants were pious and its merchants were quite cultured. Very many had gone to business schools and a good number had been graduated from a law school. But the state was run as a business proposition, and good management warned against immobilizing too many resources in humanistic culture, which was functional only to a limited extent.

The evolution from the state as a business affair to the state as a work of art, if I may still use the Burckhardtian formula, went together with the depression and the stagnation of the Renaissance. The decline of aristocracy and the recession of plutocracy left a gap through which culture, that other noblesse, could more easily shine. That culture was placed so high—higher, perhaps, than at any other period in history— is the undying glory of the Renaissance.

The transition was smooth because the seeds had been planted in the high Middle Ages. Already in the thirteenth century, culture was a creditable pastime to the nobleman and a useful asset to the merchant. It was then the fashion for kings and courtiers to write elegant lyric poems (or to have them written by the Robert Sherwoods of the time) on very

subtle matters of love and courtship. So did the merchants
who traded in and ruled over the Italian towns. They did still
more: they elaborted a formula which vaguely anticipated
the Renaissance notion that humanistic culture is the true noblesse. Real love, polite love, they said, can dwell only in a
gentle heart. Though a gentle heart is not yet the well-
rounded personality of the Renaissance, it resembles it in at
least two ways. It is unconnected with birth or riches, and it is
attainable by cultivating one's soul. Again, the Italian bourgeoisie of the thirteenth century were not content with building substantial houses with capacious storage rooms for their
merchandise and with high towers from which to pour boiling
oil on the lower towers of their neighbors. They embellished
their homes as much as they could without diminishing the
width of the storage rooms and the height of the towers. But
a merchant of the thirteenth century would have been ill
advised if he had neglected the expanding opportunities of
trade for the pursuit of humanistic culture. He was too busy
making money to consider lyric poetry and home decoration
as a fulltime occupation.

During the Renaissance many merchants were less busy
—or, at least, thought they could spare more time for culture.
In 1527 a Venetian merchant and ambassador was somewhat
shocked at seeing that in Florence "men who govern the
Republic sort and sift wool, and their sons sell cloth and
engage in other work including the lowest and dirtiest." But
this race of men was gradually dying out in Florence, as it had
in Venice. More frequently the Italian merchant princes of
the Renaissance had employees and correspondents who did
the dirtier work for them.

Let us take a great merchant, indeed the head of the
world's greatest financial organization in the fifteenth century, Lorenzo the Magnificent. He was at the same time the
head of the Medici bank, the uncrowned king of Florence,
a patron of art, and a poet in his own right. His record shows
that, unlike his medieval forefathers, he was an amateur in

business and a professional in literature. His mismangament of
the bank, or, rather, the mismanagement of the men he en-
trusted with running it, precipitated its downfall. But his
patronage of the arts gave his illegitimate power a halo of
respectability. His poems endeared him to his subjects (at
least, to those who had not been involved in the failure of the
bank) and made him famous among intellectual aristocrats
throughout the world. Niccolo Machiavelli, the great historian of Florence, lauded Lorenzo for governing the state as an
artist but blamed him for his poor conduct of business. Yet
was this shortcoming not the inevitable counterpart of his
artistic achievements? Today we no longer suffer from the
ruin of the Medici bank, while we still are enchanted by the
verse of Lorenzo de Medici. It is easier for us to be indulgent
and to observe that business at that time was so bad that even
a skilful management would not have brought many divi-
dends. Perhaps Lorenzo may be forgiven for overlooking
some opportunities to invest in trade at five per cent interest
since he invested in art at a rate which will never be ex-
hausted.

One might even contend that investment in culture drove
the Renaissance to untimely death. To obtain money for the
building of Saint Peter's in Rome, the only Renaissance
church that probably represented a greater investment in
material and manpower than any of the Gothic cathedrals,
Pope Leo X—another Medici—proclaimed a special indulgence. The sale of indulgences was the spark which ignited
the Reformation. This, indeed, was a greater and more destructive quake than the failure of the Medici bank. Still,
neither papal fiscal pressure nor popular resistance to it was a
new phenomenon. Without the investment in culture, the
split in the Christian world would probably have occurred
all the same. It is a comfort, although a meagre one, that we
have Saint Peter's as a by-product.

Every age is a blending of virtues and shortcomings. Today
we strive for unlimited human progress, and we invest colos-

sal sums in functional scientific culture. Humanistic culture does not fare equally well. Not so long ago, when the American economy was hit by a great depression, art went on WPA rolls. What a sad decline! I certainly do not advocate that the bankers of New York neglect their depositors to enrich the Metropolitan Museum. I do not even propose that our businessmen write love lyrics, or that our presidents brush up on their musical criticism. Still, would it not be a good thing if we devoted a larger proportion of our increased leisure and of our immense wealth to the fostering of humanistic culture?

BIBLIOGRAPHICAL NOTE

The traditional view of the Renaissance as a period of prosperity and economic expansion was not seriously challenged until very recent times. Some doubts were expressed by Henri Pirenne in his masterly *Economic and Social History of Medieval Europe* (Engl. transl., London, 1936) and by Gino Luzzatto in his excellent *Storia economica dell'età moderna e contemporanea,* I (2nd ed., Padua, 1938), but radical revision was chiefly the result of greater attention paid to statistical sources in the last fifteen years. The discussion of economic trends in the Renaissance was frequently in the foreground during the meetings of the Ninth International Historical Congress (Paris, 1950); see the *Rapports* and *Actes, IXe Congrès International des Sciences Historiques* (2 vols., Paris, 1950-51). Chapters IV and V in *Cambridge Economic History* II (respectively by M. M. Postan and R. S. Lopez; written in 1946 but published in 1952) are the first effort at bringing together the results of recent studies in a general reinterpretation of the Renaissance as a period of depression and stagnation. The bibliographies in that volume, p. 519-569, list the main works on the subject up to 1946.

Some of the most valuable articles and monographs which have appeared since 1946 are the following: W. Abel, *Die Wüstungen des ausgehenden Mittelalters,* Jena, 1948; C. Bardagelle, "La crisis economico-sociale dell' Italia della Rinascenza," *Nuova Rivista Storica,* XXXIV and XXXV (1950-51); R. Boutruche, *La Crise d'une société, seigneurs et paysans du Bordelais pendant la Guerre de Cent Ans,* Paris, 1947; C. M. Cipolla, "Comment s'est perdue la propriété ecclésiastique dans l'Italie du Nord," *Annales (Economies, Sociétés, Civilisations),* II, 1947; S. Lilley, *Men, Machines and History,* London, 1948; E. Perroy, "Les Crises du XIVe siecle," *Annales (Ec. S. C.),* IV, 1949; Ch. Petit-Dutaillis, *Les Communes francaises,* Paris, 1947; G. von Pölnitz, *Jakob Fugger,*

Tübingen, 1949; M. M. Postan, "Some Economic Evidence of Declining Population in the Later Middle Ages," *Economic History Review,* 2nd ser., II, 1950; R. de Roover, *The Medici Bank,* New York, 1948; J. C. Russel, *British Medieval Population,* Albuquerque, N. M., 1948; J. Schreiner, *Pest og Prisfall i Senmiddelalderen,* Oslo, 1948; N. Valeri, *Signorie e Principati,* Milan, 1950; H. van Werveke, "Essor et déclin de la Flandre," *Studi in onore di Geno Luzzatto,* I, Milan, 1950; Ph. Wolff, "Les Luttes sociales dans les villes du Midi français," *Annales* (*Ec. S. C.*), II, 1947; D. A. Zakythinos, *Crise monétaire et crise économique à Byzance,* Athens, 1948, (also in *L'Hellenisme contemporain,* I and II, 1947-48).

III THE QUEST FOR TRUTH: SCIENTIFIC PROGRESS DURING THE RENAISSANCE *by George Sarton*

Permit me to preface this lecture with a few general remarks on the history of science. Many people misunderstand science, and hence one can hardly expect them to have a fair idea of its history. The history of science might be defined as the history of the discovery of objective truth, of the gradual conquest of matter by the human mind; it describes the age-long and endless struggle for the freedom of thought—its freedom from violence, intolerance, error, and superstition.

The history of science is one of the essential parts of the spiritual history of mankind; the other main parts are the history of art and the history of religion. It differs from these other parts in that the development of knowledge is the only development which is truly cumulative and progressive. Hence, if we try to explain the progress of mankind, the history of science should be the very axis of our explanation.

Another preliminary remark is needed to define the frame of this study. It is not enough to say "the Renaissance," because that word is not understood by everybody in the same way. Let us define it as the period which elapsed between the Middle Ages and the modern age, but the Middle Ages did not end abruptly and the modern age did not begin suddenly, and their ends and beginnings were not by any means the same in different countries. Italy was ahead of the other coun-

[1] Many years ago, I took part in another symposium on the Renaissance organized by Mount Holyoke College. My contribution, "Science in the Renaissance," was included in *The Civilization of the Renaissance*, with essays by James Westfall Thompson and others, University of Chicago Press, 1929 (Ungar paperback edition now available). I have never reread it; hence this lecture is independent of it.

tries and her awakening was already begun by the middle of
the fourteenth century, in Petrarch's time. We might define
the Renaissance *grosso modo* as the period extending from
about 1350 to the death of Giordano Bruno in 1600, or to the
death of Cervantes and Shakespeare in 1616; one might
even stretch it a little further, to 1632, when Galileo published his first great book, the *Dialogo dei due massimi sistemi
del mondo.*[2] Remember that every great book of science
closes a period and opens a new one. Remember also that
no period is valid for all nations nor for the whole of any
single nation, for the men and women living at any one time
are never spiritual contemporaries. Some of our own contemporaries have not even reached the Renaissance—they are still
living in the Middle Ages; others are not even as advanced
as that; they are still living in the Stone Age. It is because of
such disparities that the progress of technology is so frighten-
ing; our ancestors were uneasy when guns were used by
children; our own fears are deeper, and we shudder to think
of atomic bombs in the hands of men who in every respect
except technology are still barbarians.

To return to the Renaissance, it was, among other things,
a revolt against medieval concepts and methods. Of course,
every generation reacts against the preceding one; every
period is a revolt against the preceding one, and so on. Yet,
in this case, the revolt was a bit sharper than it usually is.
It is not sufficiently realized that the Renaissance was not
simply a revolt against scholasticism; it was also directed
against Arabic influences (especially those represented by
Avicenna and Averroës). The anti-Arabic drive was in full
swing in Petrarch's time. Such a revolt and struggle for independence was a symptom of growing strength. In spite of
its triumph it was not completed; there are still many Arabic

[2] That *Dialogo* is, to a large extent, an epitome of Renaissance thought.
Cf. the English text edited and elucidated by Giorgio de Santillana,
University of Chicago Press, 1953, *Dialogue on the Great World
Systems.*

elements in our language and in our culture.

One of the medieval traits was the fear of novelties.[3] The Rennaissance was more tolerant of them and sometimes welcomed them, or went out of its way in order to find more of them. Each novelty created trouble, but as they impinged on the minds with increasing frequency, one got used to them and distrusted them less; one ended by liking them. In most cases, however, the novelties were rather superficial. For example, the Renaissance artists discovered the beauty of the human body, but that had never been completely forgotten.[4] They discovered the beauties of ancient art, new accents in poetry, new rhythms in music; they discovered ancient books and were anxious to publish them. All that was very exhilarating.

In the field of science, the novelties were gigantic, revolutionary. This explains why timid people are afraid of science; their instinct is sound enough; nothing can be more revolutionary than the growth of knowledge; science is at the root of every social change. The Renaissance scientists introduced not a "new look" but a new being. The novelty was often so great that one could hardly speak of a Renaissance or rebirth; it was a real birth, a new beginning.

Put it this way: The Renaissance was a transmutation of values, a "new deal," a reshuffling of cards, but most of the cards were old; the scientific Renaissance was a "new deal," but many of the cards were new. This will be shown simply and briefly as if I were to paint as quickly as possible an immense fresco. Here it is. The fresco will be divided into a dozen panels, which I shall invite you to contemplate, with indulgence, one after another.

[3] That fear was reflected in the language; for example, the Arabic word *bidca* means novelty, but it also means heresy. The Spanish word *novedad* had similar undertones.

[4] For medieval examples, see my *Introduction to the History of Science*, Vol. III, "Science and Learning in the Fourteenth Century," Williams and Wilkins, 1948, p. 1256.

I. THE DISCOVERY OF THE EARTH

Geographical discoveries were initiated by Henry the Navigator, and in this respect the Renaissance was heralded not by the Italians but by the Portuguese. Their initiative was followed gradually by other nations. It is hardly necessary to recite those heroic deeds, for everybody is familiar with them. A few names will suffice to awaken your memories: Bartholomeu Dias (1488), Christopher Columbus (1492), Vasco da Gama (1498), Amerigo Vespucci (1497-1504), Ferdinand Magellan (1519-22), etc. The Renaissance was truly the golden age of geographical discovery; by the year 1600 the surface of the known earth was doubled. Was not that an achievement of incredible pregnancy? The earth was doubled! It was not only a matter of quantity, but one of quality as well. New climates, new aspects of nature were revealed.

Ancient and medieval navigations had been largely coastal; mariners seldom spent many days without sight of land. They knew the seas, but now they had conquered the oceans; they learned to know the arctic regions, the deserts, and the tropics.

Each of us can measure those novelties, for if he searches his own mind, he may be able to recapture the deep emotions which he felt when he found himself for the first time in the middle of the ocean, or in the heart of a tropical jungle, or when he tried to cross a desert or glacier. These discoveries, which are fundamental for each of us individually, were made for the whole of mankind in the fifteenth and sixteenth centuries.

We are all aware of those geographical discoveries which added new continents and innumerable islands to our estates, but relatively few people realize that new aspects of nature were discovered in the very heart of Europe, that is, the high Alps, which earlier men had been afraid of exploring. This was a new world within the heart of the old. The severity and danger of the Alpine climate had deluded medieval minds into believing that the high mountains were the abode

of gnomes and devils. In this they were less advanced than
the Buddhists of India, China, and Japan, who regarded the
mountains as sacred, and built temples on their slopes and at
the very tops. The earliest Alpine expeditions began very
timidly in the fourteenth century, but did not assume any
importance before the sixteenth century; by the end of that
century some forty-seven summits had been reached.[5] Two
main purposes could be served in Alpine expeditions; the first
was aesthetic or religious, the second was scientific. One might
risk one's life in difficult ascents in order to enjoy the beauty
of nature and the sublimity of God, or in order to understand
the mysterious climate obtaining at high altitudes, and to
observe the shape of the mountains and the plants and animals that inhabited them. The first man to combine in himself both purposes was Leonardo da Vinci.

II. THE NEW EDUCATION

Any renaissance must express itself in the field of education, for when men begin to think and feel in a new way
they are eager to modify teaching methods in proportion to
their own spiritual change. Unfortunately, the great majority
of schools were informal and the teacher of genius could
hardly emerge from the local and temporal circumstances
which limited his activities. For example, the *Casa giocosa*
established by Vittorino da Feltre in Mantua in 1423 did not
surivive him. The same remark might be made about great
educators like the Catalan, Juan Luis Vives (1492-1540),
and the Englishman, Roger Ascham (1515-68). New peda-
gogical ideas cannot be effective unless incorporated in an
educational system of some permanence.

A development of greater stability had been begun in the

[5] The first treatise *ad hoc* was that of Josias Simler: *De Alpibus*
(Zürich, 1574). It is a very curious fact that Alpinism stopped at the
end of the sixteenth century and did not begin again in earnest until the
end of the eighteenth century.

meantime by the Brothers of the Common Life in the Netherlands, at the very end of the fourteenth century. By the way, this is another aspect of the early Renaissance which is not Italian. Its importance can hardly be exaggerated. The *Devotio moderna* was an attempt to reconcile the humanities with Christianity. This could be done only on a mystical plane, but the Dutch Brothers did it very well, and their influence spread rapidly in northwestern Europe. By the middle of the fifteenth century there were already some 150 of their schools in the Netherlands, France, and Germany, and those schools remained the best of their kind until the sixteenth century. Many great men were educated by the Brothers of the Common Life, the two most famous ones being Cardinal Nicolaus of Cusa (1401-64), who loved them, and Erasmus of Rotterdam (1466-1536), who was irritated by them. By Erasmus' time the schools had lost their spiritual power; in the second half of the sixteenth century they were replaced and eclipsed by the Jesuit colleges.

Much credit for the educational revival must be given also to the reformers. From the Protestant point of view, a modicum of education was a religious duty. Every Christian should be able to read the Scriptures by himself. Therefore, Martin Luther was very deeply concerned with public education. In 1524, Magdeburg organized new schools on the plan which he had recommended. Other schools were established in many German cities, and their availability to the children was gradually increased; it has been claimed that the public school system of the German Protestant states was the first model of our own. The inspirer and organizer of that system was Philip Melanchthon (1497-1560), whose influence was so pervading and lasting that he fully deserved the title given to him, *Praeceptor Germaniae.*

III. THE NEW MATHEMATICS

Historians of art never fail to discuss the new conception of perspective which was largely due to Florentine artists but which grew also in Flanders and Germany. This implied a certain amount of mathematical thinking, but that amount was very small, almost negligible. The new mathematics which we have in mind is something more profound and infinitely more complex. We will refer only to its main aspects, for the references are almost meaningless except for mathematical students. The history of mathematical ideas is peculiarly difficult to explain (even to mathematicians), because the first achievements were made in Babylonia, matured in Greece, incubated in the Arabaic world, and gradually reappeared in the West. The astonishing flowering of the fifteenth and sixteenth centuries concerned trigonometry and algebra. Trigonometry was revived by Germans like Regiomontanus (1436-76), then by Georg Joachim Rheticus (1514-76) and Bartholomaeus Pitiscus; algebra by Italians, like Scipione del Ferro, Nicola Tartaglia, Girolamo Cardano (1501-76), and Lodovico Ferrari. The gradual introduction of a number of operational symbols prepared the writing of equations as we do, and the theory of equations began to take shape. The climax of Renaissance mathematics was reached by such men as the Italian, Raffaele Bombelli (fl. 1572), the Frenchman, François Viète (1540-1603), and the Fleming, Simon Stevinus (1548-1620). In 1585, Stevin published his invention of decimal fractions and decimal weights and measures. He then explained with great lucidity an idea which the Anglo-Saxon world has not been able to grasp to this day.

These mathematical discoveries were not as tangible as the geographical ones; yet they were deeper. The Conquistadores were very materialistic, greedy and inhuman; the mathematicians were the opposite in every respect and their conquests were spiritual ones, conquests of pure reason, the scope of which was infinite.

IV. THE NEW ASTRONOMY

Now let us travel to Frombork in Poland, where Copernicus was ending his days in 1543. His great treatise, the first copy of which was brought to him on his deathbed, explained the new astronomy. It was not radically new, for the fundamental idea of it had been outlined before by Aristarchus of Samos during another Renaissance (the Hellenistic Renaissance of Alexandria). Yet, Aristarchus' views had been rejected by the leading astronomers of antiquity and had been driven underground. To re-explain them, as Copernicus did after more than eighteen centuries of discredit, was very much the same as a new creation. The sun was put back in the center of the world, and the earth reduced to a planetary status. The implications of this theory, as set forth by Giordano Bruno and others, were not simply of astronomical interest, but of philosophical importance. It is a strange paradox that at the very time when man was beginning to conquer nature, he was obliged to drive himself away from the center of things; in proportion as he grew wiser he had to make himself smaller. That is all right, of course. The purpose of science is to discover the truth irrespective of consequences.

It is pleasant to recall that Copernicus was helped in his computations by a much younger man, Georg Joachim Rheticus, who visited him and lived with him for more than two years. In 1539, when Rheticus arrived, he was only 25, while Copernicus was 66. The main point is this: Copernicus was a canon of the Cathedral of Frombork, while Rheticus was a professor in the Protestant University of Wittenberg. At a time when the hatred dividing Catholics from Protestants was getting as hot as hellfire, the old canon and the young Protestant mathematician were living and working together like brothers. Science is not simply international, it is almost always *au dessus de la mêlée*; it unites all men in a sublime task, the quest for truth. It may be added that in the sixteenth century Catholic and Protestant theologians were united in one common hatred, their hatred of the Copernican theory, which conflicted with the Scriptures.

Copernicus was a poor observer and it had been easier for him (as it had been for Aristarchus) to formulate his new theory, because he was not embarrassed by good observations. (Science proceeds by successive approximations; if the early astronomers had been given excellent telescopes, they would have been so bewildered that they would have been unable to understand anything.) The new vision which had been opened by Copernicus warmed the enthusiasm of a Danish boy, Tycho Brahe (1546-1601), who was to become one of the best astronomical observers of all time. He was able to accumulate a large mass of observations which were more accurate than his simple instruments seemed to warrant, but these observations increased his perplexities, and he felt obliged to abandon the heliocentric hypothesis (even as Hipparchus had felt obliged to do seventeen centuries before him) and to adopt a kind of compromise. This was not the first time (nor the last) that careful observations drove out a theory which was good, but not good enough, and required some corrections in order to be admissible. The final establishment of the Copernican theory by Johann Kepler (1609, 1619) is outside our frame, yet the fact remains that Copernicus was the first to formulate it without equivocation. This he did in 1543.

Many medieval astronomers had realized the growing inadequacy of the Julian calendar, but their claims for reform had remained unheeded. Pope Gregory XIII, helped by the Bavarian mathematician, Christopher Clavius, and buoyed up by the spirit of novelty which informed his time, finally accomplished the much needed reform. The "novelty" was less profound than that of the Copernican theory, but it was more tangible to the mass of the people. The good Catholics who went to sleep on October 4, 1582, woke up the next morning on October 15. That was startling enough, was it not? But the surprise was restricted to Catholics. The reform had come just too late; if it had been decided upon before the Reformation, the whole of Latin Christendom would have accepted it without demur. At this time, however, self-respecting Protestants could not receive a new calendar from the hands of their chief adversary. Therefore, they continued to use the Julian calendar (in England until as late as 1752), and one could already have taunted them with Voltaire's sarcasm: Those idiots "prefer to disagree with the sun than to agree with the Pope."

V. THE NEW PHYSICS AND CHEMISTRY

Changes in physics were less radical than in other fields, and the situation of chemistry was even more confused. The medieval incubation of mechanical ideas was not by any means completed. We owe many little clarifications to Italians like Tartaglia, Cardano, Benedetti, Guido Ubaldo; but the ablest clarifier before Galileo was the Fleming, Simon Stevinus. Stevinus, the greatest mechanician in the nineteen centuries between Archimedes and Galileo, introduced new ideas into statics and into hydrostatics.

In the meantime, the intense rivalries of colonizing nations encouraged the progress of navigation and of the physical sciences which would increase the accuracy of sailings and minimize their dangers. The main requirements were geodetic, astronomic (better methods of taking the ship's bearings), cartographic; one needed faster ships and better instruments to navigate them. Geodetic improvements were due to the Frenchman, Jean Fernel, and the Dutchman, Gemma Frisius; better maps to the Portuguese, Pedro Nuñez, and the Flemings, Gerhard Mercator and Abraham Ortelius. Who has not seen the splendid geographic atlases which were produced in the sixteenth century? Not only did they provide a large mass of information of vital importance to statesman and merchants; some of their maps were so beautiful that it is a joy to look at them.

One of the first fruits of oceanic navigation was a better knowledge of magnetic declination, for the compass was one of the sailor's best instruments, but its readings could not be trusted without taking occasional deviations into account. The magnetic observations and other knowledge useful for navigation were put together by Englishmen like Robert Norman (1581) and William Barlow (1597) and by Simon Stevinus (1599). At the very end of the Renaissance, William Gilbert published the first great treatise on magnetism (1600); it is significant that his knowledge of terrestrial magnetism, rudimentary as it still was, induced him to outline cosmological implications.

In optics the best work was done by Italians like Giovanni Battista della Porta (1538?-1615) and Maurolycus, but progress was not very tangible. In spite of the fact that so few physical (and chemical) phenomena could be accounted for in rational terms, the results were so alluring that the investigators were full of conceit. They were aware of the nearness of mysteries the penetration of which might expose them to suspicion. Della Porta's famous book was entitled *Magia naturalis* (1538). Various little academies were founded in Italy during the sixteenth century; they were somewhat in the nature of exclusive clubs and secret societies; the members were often known to each other by nicknames; their academies offered them means of discussing the elusive "secrets" which they hoped and feared to disclose. At any rate, they gave them privacy and protection against the misunderstandings of the ignorant and the bigots.

Physical "secrets" included chemical ones, but in the field of chemistry the fundamental ideas were even more difficult to separate and to define. Vision and understanding were obscured by alchemical fancies around which had gathered all kinds of superstitions. The defeat of alchemy was not really begun until the end of the seventeenth century, and its completion required still another century of patient work. In the Renaissance it was out of the question, and historians of chemistry look upon that period as the golden age of alchemy.

VI. THE NEW TECHNOLOGY

The only branch of technology which has never become inactive is the art of warfare. In this age, as in all others, most technicians were concerned with that art, trying to find new weapons, to improve the old ones, or to defend themselves more effectively against the weapons of their enemies. The invention of new arms and new armor was always the main obsession of men, good or bad.[6] Even as great an artist and as serene a man as Leonardo da Vinci was obliged to devote much of his attention to such problems. Yet the greatest invention of the Renaissance was a peaceful one: the invention of typography. It is hardly necessary to indicate what the art of printing meant for the diffusion of culture, but one should not lay too much stress on diffusion and should speak more of standardization. Every manuscript was in many respects unique. Printing made it possible for the first time to publish hundreds of copies that were alike and yet might be scattered everywhere. It was now possible (as it had never been before) to refer to a definite statement made on page X of such and such a book; the reference made by a scholar in Oxford might be checked immediately by his colleagues in Salamanca, in Bruges, or in Vienna. Steady advance implies the exact determination of every previous step; this now became incomparably easier. That "divine art," as the early typographers did not hesitate to call it, was invented about the middle of the fifteenth century in Germany. Thus we see once more that the early Renaissance was not exclusively Italian; the most pregnant initiatives were taken far away from Italy—in Portugal, in Holland, and in Germany.

The invention of typography was considerably enriched by the invention of engraving, which was accomplished and

[6] A list of early treatises on war technology is given in my *Introduction to the History of Science*, Vol. III, "Science and Learning in the Fourteenth Century," pp. 1550-54. Those technicians were Germans or Italians.

vulgarized at about the same time. Woodcuts and copper-plates did for the graphic arts exactly what printing did for letters. Works of art could be diffused and standardized. The two inventions, printing and engraving, were of immense importance for the development of knowledge. Printing made possible the publication of mathematical and astronomical tables which could be depended upon; engraving, the publication of books with illustrations representing plants, animals, anatomical or surgical details, chemical apparatus, etc. One good figure is more revealing than many pages of text; the use of illustrations obliged the author to be more precise than he could have been, or wished to be, without them.

The new technology was symbolized by the publication of illustrated treatises by Vannoccio Biringuccio of Siena (1540), Georgius Agricola (1556), Lazarus Ercker (1574), all of which included a wealth of information on mining, metallurgy, chemistry, the founding of guns and bells, the making of weapons and gunpowder, the casting of alloys such as type metal, the coining of money, and many other arts and crafts. This suggests that, thanks to printing and engraving, the Renaissance was a vigorous age of stocktaking and encyclopaedism as well as of invention. Every bit of knowledge could now be garnered and preserved forever. Words and images were immortalized.

VII. THE NEW BOTANY

One aspect of the Renaissance has often been described and emphasized: the publication of the Latin and Greek classics, many of which had been lost because they were represented by single manuscripts, which were buried and forgotten in the corners of neglected libraries. The discovery of such manuscripts was as thrilling as the discovery today of papyri or clay tablets. There were incunabular editions of the great botanical books of antiquity, those of Theophrastus and Dioscorides, but those early editions were not illustrated. The descriptions of plants, even when correct, were confusing, because they referred to another flora than that of western Europe. In this case, the classics had to be rejected and the work of botanical description done over. The pioneers, "the fathers of botany," were Germans like Otto Brunfels (1530), Leonhard Fuchs (1542), Hieronymus Bock, and Valerius Cordus; and they were followed by Flemings like Dodonaeus, Clusius, Lobelius, Busbecq, by Englishmen, Italians, etc. Not only were new herbals illustrated but some of the illustrations were very beautiful.

Botany was then an essential part of medical teaching, and the use of illustrated herbals intensified the need of direct observations. The ancient botanists had been satisfied mostly with names, an abundance of synonyms, and the enumeration of qualities or virtues; the German "fathers" and their followers had added images; now there was a growing desire to see and handle the plants themselves. Botanical gardens were attached to the medical schools (the first university garden was in Padua, 1545); dried plants were collected in herbaria by Luca Ghini (who died in Bologna in 1556) and by many others. A new botanical knowledge was within reach, and brisk emulation caused it to grow rapidly in a great many places.

VIII.   THE NEW ZOOLOGY (AND MINERALOGY)

Animals were studied in the same spirit as plants, and students of natural history were stimulated by the discovery of new countries beyond the seas, where plants and animals were either radically new, or sufficiently different from those already known, to be startling, to cause perplexities, and to invite further investigations. There emerged a new kind of scientist, the traveling naturalist, the scientific explorer. The greedy adventurers of early days were now replaced by men in search of knowledge. The quest for truth inspired them with a missionary zeal, and they were prepared to suffer many hardships for the sake of science.

The discoveries made in foreign lands excited the naturalists who were obliged to stay at home, such as physicians, professors, and the keepers of botanical gardens and greenhouses, and necessitated their describing more accurately and more completely the faunas and floras of their own countries. Thus exploration abroad caused deeper investigations and led to better knowledge of all the forms of life which could be observed nearer home.

I should also like to mention the mineralogical investigations. Some minerals were generally included in the early herbals, and the search for mineral drugs was increased in the sixteenth century. The main mineralogical work, however, was done and had always been done by prospectors in search of rich ores. This was part of the business of mining, such as was described in *De re metallica* of Agricola (1556), mentioned above. The collectors of precious stones had never stopped their activities, and their business was roused when more gold and silver was mined in Europe and America.

By 1600 the knowledge of the three kingdoms of nature was radically different from what it had been in the Middle Ages; it was incomparably richer, and, what matters even more, it was more genuine; a larger proportion of it was based on direct observations. This does not mean, unfortunately, that all the early fantasies had been eliminated; the average Renaissance naturalist was able to make good observations, and he became abler to make better ones every year, but few of them were strong enough to reject deeply-rooted superstitions. The amount of information, old and new, genuine or not, was so enormous by the second half of the sixteenth century that it made necessary the encyclopaedic efforts of Konrad von Gesner of Zürich and of Ulisse Aldrovandi of Bologna.

IX. THE NEW ANATOMY

The new anatomy was created by Leonardo da Vinci and by Andreas Vesalius of Brussels. Leonardo was not an amateur anatomist, as so many artists were, but an indefatigable investigator who spent more time in elaborate dissections than most professionals. He examined almost every organ of the human body, taking copious notes and making admirable drawings; yet all that work was kept in his archives and remained practically unknown until the last century. On the other hand, Vesalius published in 1543 his *Fabrica,* which became known at once and which marks the beginning of a new era in anatomical studies. Mark that the same year, 1543, was the era of the new anatomy as well as of the new astronomy; it was one of the golden years of the Renaissance.

X. THE NEW MEDICINE

Among many great physicians it must suffice in this brief outline to mention three who were outstanding in their respective lines, true pioneers who represent three different countries: the Swiss, Paracelsus, the Italian, Girolamo Fracastoro, and the Frenchman, Ambroise Paré.

Paracelsus of Einsiedeln, near Zürich, is the best exemplar of the new medicine which had not yet completely emerged from medieval confusion. At his best, he was a pioneer in many directions—in the study of mental diseases, as the founder of iatro-chemistry (chemistry applied to medicine), and as the distant herald of homeopathy. He was an adventurous experimentalist, yet his sounder views were crudely mixed with metaphysical and magical ideas, and his rational cures could not always be separated from miraculous ones. His study of the diseases of miners was the first to be devoted to occupational or industrial medicine. He was original to the point of extravagance, indiscreet and bombastic, generous and foolish—a kind of medical gypsy, restless and dogmatic, a man of genius, a great doctor, and a charlatan.

The scientific fame of Fracastoro of Verona rests mainly on his treatise on contagion (1546), in which he suggested that infection is caused by the transmission, from a person who is diseased to one who is healthy, of minute bodies capable of self-multiplication. This was an adumbration of modern theories (it could not be more than that before the discovery of microscopes and much else). His popular fame was based on another book of his to which we shall refer presently.

Ambroise Paré (1510-90) was a military surgeon whose native genius had not been inhibited by the scholastic medical education of his time and by irrelevant Latin learning; he was able, therefore, to take full advantage of every one of his innumerable observations with an open mind. He introduced so many novelties that he may be called the founder of modern surgery. His modesty was equal to his experience; it is well illustrated by a familiar statement of his: *"Je le pansai, Dieu le guerit"* (I dressed his wound, God healed it).

These three great men reveal the complexity of the Renaissance, for they were as different as they could be: Paracelsus the rebel, Fracastoro the classicist, Paré the wise practitioner. Paracelsus' genius was still in many respects medieval, Fracastoro's ancient, Paré's modern; yet they were children of the same century.

XI. NEW DISEASES

It was not enough for the Renaissance to have great physicians; the age indulged itself in new diseases. When we said above that one might consider the middle of the fourteenth century as its starting point, we were not thinking only of Petrarch and Boccaccio and of the new culture which they symbolized, but also of the Black Death, whose first outburst (1348-52) was so terrible that one fourth of the population was destroyed and another fourth at least completely demoralized. This was perhaps the most frightful calamity of its kind in history, and it was of such extent and rigor that one could hardly find a better dividing line between the old age (the Middle Ages) and the new one. The Black Death did not stop in 1352; it flared up repeatedly throughout the fourteenth century and later. It was not, however, even in 1348, a new disease, but simply the worst example of a very old one.

The Renaissance suffered two other diseases which were peculiarly its own. The first, the physical, was syphilis; the second, mental, was the fear of witchcraft.

Syphilis made so dramatic an appearance at the siege of Naples in 1495 that it is difficult to resist the conclusion that it was really a new disease imported from the new world. That hypothesis cannot be completely proved,[7] but it is strengthened by two sets of considerations. In the first place, syphilis has very definite symptoms, and it is hard to believe that all of the great physicians of the past would have overlooked them if they had been present. There is no mention of those symptoms and no description of any disease suggesting syphilis in the abundant medical writings anterior to 1495, in Greek, Arabic, and Latin. In the second place, the explosive development of syphilis at the end of the fifteenth century suggests that it was a new disease for which Europeans were utterly unprepared.[8] The lack of syphilis literature before 1495 was compensated by its abundance afterwards.

The most remarkable publication *ad hoc* was the Latin poem written by Fracastoro in 1531, if only because it was that poem which gave its name to that disease (after the romantic shepherd Syphilus, who contracted it).[9] Fracastoro's poem enjoyed considerable popularity. The author's main intention was to sing the praise of a new remedy *guaiacan*

[7] The literature concerning the origin of syphilis is immense and never ceases to grow, with every year a few more books or papers on the subject being published.

[8] In the same way, smallpox, introduced by Europeans into America, destroyed a very large number of Indians (*Isis* 37, 124). Many other examples could be adduced concerning not only human diseases, but also plant and animal pests.

[9] Syphilis is the only disease having a poetic name.

(*guaiacum, lignum sanctum,* holy wood). The discovery of that wonderful drug (as it was thought to be at the beginning) confirms the American origin of the disease. According to a medieval conceit, God had placed remedies close to the diseases which they could cure, counter-poisons near the poisons, etc. Now, if syphilis came from the West Indies, it was natural to hunt for a drug in that part of the world. This was done and the herb duly found; it was the one which the Indians called in their language *guaiacan.*

The German humanist, Ulrich von Hutten (1488-1523), who had cured himself with *guaiacan,* wrote a treatise on the subject (1519) which he dedicated to the Archbishop of Mainz. At the end of it he did not scruple to say something like this: "I hope that Your Eminence has escaped the pox, but should you catch it (Heaven forbid, but one can never tell) I would be glad to treat and cure you." This is another typical Renaissance trait. The good archbishop realized that no offense was meant and took none. Syphilis was then a terrible disease (more terrible than now), but it was not considered more disgraceful than other diseases, and it caused less hypocrisy than it does today.

The other disease, much more terrible than syphilis, was the fear of witchcraft which became virulent at about the same time. The virulence was caused by a bull of Innocent VIII (1484) and exacerbated by the *Malleus maleficarum* (1486). This was a treatise written for the guidance of inquisitors; it explained how to detect, convict, and punish the witches. Looking at it from our point of view it might be considered a textbook of sexual psychopathology. The fear of witches caused their persecution, and the persecutions increased the fears. There appeared and spread everywhere a mass psychosis the like of which was not experienced again until our own days. The procedure followed in many witch trials was scrupulously recorded, and therefore we are very well informed. Many witches confessed their crimes and described their association with the Devil; their descriptions of the latter tally so often that one might take them as an objective proof of his reality. These poor women who were burned to death were neurotics whom we would send to hospitals. The witchcraft delusion could not be cured by theologians, who could detect only sin and heresy; it was instead a matter for physicians who recognized pathological conditions. The first physician to see that was the Dutchman Johann Weyer, who cannot be praised too highly for doing what he did as early as 1563.[10]

These medical subjects have been dealt with at greater length than the others because they are both easy to describe and because they illustrate some aspects of the Renaissance less glorious than the usual ones, yet essential for its understanding. The sixteenth century was a golden age of the humanities and of art, but it was also an age of intolerance[11] and cruelty; it sometimes proved itself inhuman to a degree hardly surpassed at any time except our own.

XII. THE NEW ARTS

To return to more pleasant aspects (we must recognize the gloomy parts, though it is unwise to dwell on them overmuch), the quest for truth was so continuous and fervent and it was carried on by so many great men of many nations that mankind approached much closer to its goal, and at greater speed, than had been possible in medieval times. The consequences of that quest can be observed in every kind of endeavor, whether material or spiritual.

[10] For more information on this very great man see *Isis* 25, 147-52, 1936.

[11] I have not discussed the wars between Catholics and Protestants which disgraced Europe and Christendom because that would have taken me too far aside. The repressions of witchcraft and heresy were often confused by the inquisitors, and more so by the public. We should be indulgent, because similar delusions and confessions disgrace our own times. However, everything considered, it is not quite as disgraceful to kill one another in the name of Marx as to do so in the name of Christ.

What could be more appropriate for our example than the field of art? Take perspective. That was in a sense a mathematical subject, but its adaptation to drawing and painting was realized in the fifteenth century by a number of artists: Filippo Brunelleschi, Leone Battista Alberti, Paolo Uccello, Piero della Francesca, Leonardo da Vinci (all of them Tuscan or closely connected with Florence). The first two were architects, and it is hardly necessary to point out the many connections between architecture, on the one hand, and mathematics, physics, and engineering, on the other. The architectural renaissance implied a scientific renaissance. The painters needed not only the new geometrical (or linear) perspective; they needed also the subtler knowledge to which the Middle Ages had given the same ambiguous name, perspective—aerial perspective, we call it. This was a mixture of optics, meteorology, and theory of shades and colors. With regard to this, artists received some assistance from men of science, but the best work in the West was done by Leonardo da Vinci. In their fresh enthusiasm for the beauty of human forms the artists needed some knowledge of anatomy, and here again Leonardo was their outstanding guide. Other tasks required the help of geographers, geologists, mineralogists, naturalists, and in this case the best exemplar (aside from Leonardo) was the Frenchman, Bernard Palissy.

To return to art and science, the need of both and the feeling for both, the most illustrious representatives of that ambivalence are the Florentine, Leonardo da Vinci (1452-1519), and Albrecht Dürer (1471-1528) of Nuremberg. They were contemporaries, the second a little younger than the first; but they did not meet, nor did they influence each other to any degree. Being children of the same eld, their scientific problems were the same, but Dürer devoted more time to art, and Leonardo to science. Leonardo was a better scientist and a deeper philosopher than Dürer. He was, above all, a great anatomist and a great technician; he invented many machines, but (this is almost incredible) he paid no attention to the

greatest inventions of his age (indeed, of all ages), printing
and engraving. On the other hand, Dürer, being a practical
man, a man of business, was one of the first to exploit both inventions. He created hundreds of woodcuts and engravings,
and three books were written, illustrated, engraved, printed,
and published by him. Leonardo was a dreamer and, from the
world's point of view, a failure; Dürer was a very successful
man. I can admire them both, but I love Leonardo. He was
the finest flower of the Renaissance, the best illustration of
that radiant age in two respects: the first is the one indicated
by the very name Renaissance—rebirth, novelty (everybody
appreciates that); the second is the realization, more complete
in him than in any other man, that art and science, the pursuit
of beauty and the pursuit of truth, are two complementary
undertakings. The personality of Leonardo was so over-
whelming that it embraced many Oriental elements as well as
western ones, another reason why he merits our admiration
and gratitude. Leonardo saw clearly five hundred years ago
what very few people are able to see today, and the few who
do see it can do so only because they stand on his shoulders.

A final remark. General as it has been, my account has
brought to light, among other things, the fact that the quest
for knowledge has always been international or supranational,
even more fundamentally so than the quest for beauty. The
Italians could have created all of their masterpieces just as
well if the Germans, the Flemings, and the English had not
existed. On the other hand, scientific discoveries always implied the collaboration of many nations. No scientific achievement can ever be explained within the limits of a single
country. Had I dealt also with India, China, and Japan, I
would have shown many curious relationships, but I have
hardly been able here to do justice to the West alone. But
the main problems of life cannot be solved by men of
science alone, nor by artists and humanists. We need the co-
operation of all of them. Science is always necessary, never
sufficient; we are starving for beauty, and where charity is
lacking, nothing else is of any avail.

IV MAN, GOD, AND THE CHURCH IN THE AGE OF THE RENAISSANCE

by Roland H. Bainton

The Renaissance is currently conceived to have been at variance with the Middle Ages and nowhere more so than in the area of religion. The classic contrast was vividly drawn by Symonds. He took, as his type of the Middle Ages, St. Bernard, who rode for an entire day beside the shores of Lake Leman without "noticing the azure of the waters, the radiance of the mountains with their robe of sun and snow, but instead bent his thought-burdened forehead over the neck of his mule, and at the end of the journey, when his companions referred to the lake, inquired, 'What lake?' Even so were the men of that day pilgrims intent on sin, death, and judgment. They esteemed beauty a snare, pleasure a sin, the world a fleeting show, man as depraved, judgment inevitable, hell everlasting, and heaven best attained by the mortification of the flesh."[1]

The type of the Renaissance was Dr. Faustus, an emancipated Dr. Faustus, for in the original tale the devil played a part and to him the doctor had to pledge his soul in order that blind Homer might sing for him, that at his behest Alexander might rise from the dead with all his legionaries, and Helen of Troy be given to him as a bride. That for which Faustus forfeited his soul the Renaissance appropriated without price. "Homer, no longer by the intervention of a fiend but by the labor of the scholar, sang to the new age." The legions of Alexander rose again in the pages of the historians, and Helen was taken to wife in the recovery of the ineffable beauty of Greek art, of which her loveliness was the symbol. Not by magic but by the toilsome devotion to erudition on the part of magnificent Italy was the guilty dream of the ancient

[1] J. A. Symonds, *The Renaissance in Italy*: "The Age of the Despots," 1935 (Capricon paperback edition available), pp. 9-10.

legend given blithe fulfillment; and thereby was ushered in the modern world.[2]

This picture like many another interpretation of the past has of late been subjected to revision. There are those who point out that the Middle Ages were not innocent of the Faustian type. There were Aucassins who, with a Nicolette and a convivial company of lords and dames, preferred hell to a bored eternity with stuffy saints. There were roistering vagabond students, throat-cutting outlaws, predatory barons, and wenching bishops. Contemporary with St. Bernard was Abelard, the troubadour theologian tinctured with rationalism.

On the other hand, there were Bernards in the age of the Renaissance. Michelangelo could never dismiss from memory the reverberations of the diluvian tones of Savonarola as he stunned his hearers with predictions of imminent doom. Nor should one forget the renown of San Bernardino of Siena, nor of that other Bernardino, also of Siena, known as Ochino, the general of the Capuchins of the order of St. Francis, who toured Italy on penitential missions, barefoot, meanly clad, emaciated, his long white beard and ethereal countenance reminiscent of the face of Moses after he had talked with God. And all this in the very heyday of Renaissance in the Eternal City. Even the humanists, of the first generation at least, were imbued with the ideals of Franciscan poverty and regarded as their patron St. Jerome, the monastic scholar.[3]

One is prompted to wonder whether Bernard and Faust are not perhaps eternal contemporaries existing side by side in every age and culture. To go so far, however, would be to abandon differentiation of historical periods; and some shifts

[2] *Ibid.*, "The Revival of Learning," 1935 (Capricorn paperback edition now available) p. 354. The Faust story emerges full-blown only at the end of the sixteenth century, and even then not in Symonds' emancipated form. Stories of compacts with the devil are common in the Middle Ages.

[3] Hans Baron, "Franciscan Poverty and Civil Wealth in Humanistic Thought," *Speculum* XIII, 1, Jan. 1938, pp. 1-37.

of emphasis and interest certainly are evident.

These two types afford a contrast all the more striking because there are so many parallels to be compared. Both in-
volve man's behavior, his concept of himself, his aspirations
declared or unavowed, his belief as to his destiny and as to
those forces which brought him into being and determine or
contend for his fate.

We may conveniently begin with man, the way in which
he demeaned himself and the manner in which he envisaged
his place and role in the universe. The classic portrayal has
thought to find in the Renaissance the emergence of the
superman, egoistic, ambitious, unscrupulous, ruthless, and re-
morseless, consumed with a passion not for immortality but
for fame. The type is seen in the despots of the Italian city
states. Take for example Fondolo of Cremona who, when the
Pope and the emperor visited him on their way to the Council
of Constance, took them to the rampart of a high tower afford-
ing a view of the panorama of the Po. The thought flashed
into the mind of Fondolo that here was a remarkable opportunity to immortalize himself by pushing them both over
the parapet, thus attaining the distinction of having killed a
pope and an emperor on the same day. He resisted the tempta-
tion, but when later he himself was condemned to execution,
regretted that he had let pass the greatest opportunity of his
life.[4] And then there were all the Sforzas, Viscontis, the
Medici, and the Borgias, whose demeanor supplied the models
for Machiavelli's *Prince*. Al Capones were they in the methods by which they won and held power, but Carnegies, Rocke-
fellers, and Morgans in the liberality with which they
employed it. The distinction of these elegant banditti is to be
found less in their buccaneering behavior—that can be
matched in other periods—than in their patronage of the
arts. Lorenzo de Medici was equally adept in plotting an as-
sassination, making merry at a carnival, or in judging a horse,

[4] J. A. Symonds, "The Age of the Despots," p. 233, note 17.

a sermon, a poem, or a picture, and this it is that marks him off from ordinary cutthroats.

Perhaps then we should shift from the lust for power to the love of elegance as the primary note of the era. The ideal was the rounding out of man's personality, the development of all his capacities, the subjection of all disciplines to his rational control. The courtier literature draws the picture of the well-rounded man. He can fight, dance, swim, hunt, woo, and warble. His mind introduces system into every field. War becomes strategy, business is bookkeeping, statecraft is diplomacy, art is perspective. Here and now man aspires to bring to bloom his seeded powers and cherishes less a blessed immortality than an imperishable name acquired not by spectacular deviltry but by artistic and literary pre-eminence. One thinks at this point of the burgeoning geniuses of the Renaissance: Leonardo in art and mechanics; Michelangelo in painting, sculpture, and architecture; Rabelais in medicine and literature; Raleigh in exploration and historiography; Servetus in theology and physiology; Postel in statecraft, mathematics, and orientalia; Erasmus in classical and patristic scholarship, not to mention journalism. Many of them were supported by a Maecenas who thought to attain an undying reputation through his protégé's dedication. Surely here we have a contrast to the prevailing anonymity of medieval donors and craftsmen who vied with one another to honor the Blessed Virgin without carving their names into the pediments.

Even more, we are told, is this the period in which man had the temerity first to apply to himself a designation hitherto reserved for God, the title of creator. The sculptors, painters, and poets first commenced to talk of their "creations." To point the comparison, God himself was painted seated at an easel. All of the modern vocabulary of creative art, creative writing, creative painting stems thus from the Renaissance.[5] The Middle Ages would have regarded such terminology as

[5] Edgar Zilsel, *Die Entstehung des Geniebegriffes* (1926), pp. 280-83.

arrogant, if not indeed well-nigh blasphemous. Did not Thomas Aquinas say, "God alone can create, because creation is the bringing of something out of nothing, and that no man can ever do"?[6]

This total picture may not be wholly without warrant. A certain shift of tone is discernible in the Renaissance, but the differences can be grossly exaggerated. The *uomo universale* was for some indeed an ideal, and yet he may also have been simply the result of a lack of specialization, just as in the early nineteenth century Benjamin Silliman handled both chemistry and geology because the sciences were not yet sufficiently advanced to compel a division. Again, the claim of newness for the application to man of the title "creator" calls for considerable qualification. The view of Aquinas was not that which prevailed in antiquity, for the doctrine of creation out of nothing was a scholastic invention. It is not the classical Greek view as expounded in the *Timaeus,* nor even the Hebrew picture of the first chapter of Genesis, where the Spirit of God brooded over the waters and the waters were already there. The Greeks did not hesitate to apply to man two of the words descriptive of God as Creator. The one was *Demiourgos* and the other was *Poetes.* Nor did St. Paul himself disdain this latter term. The position of Thomas Aquinas was not even that of the other scholastics, for he frankly avowed that at this point he was dissenting from the *Magister Sententiarum* (even as now the author of this article ventures to dissent from the *Magister Omnium Artium et Scientiarum,* Erwin Panofsky). Peter Lombard had said that in the absolute sense, to be sure, creation cannot be predicated of man. No more can the forgiveness of sins; yet in a derivative sense man may be said both to create and to forgive.[7] Aquinas, in taking issue with him, objected only to his terminology. He would reserve strictly for God the designation "creator," and would apply

[6] Summa Theol. I, 45, 8.
[7] Sent. II, I and IV, 5.

to man rather the title "concreator."[8] The Renaissance then did not so much introduce a new view of man as display a distaste for overly refined distinctions.

If one turns to the doctrine of man as expounded by Renaissance writers, the departure from the classical Christian picture is evident but not glaring. Let us examine three cases. Take first the passage most frequently cited as marking the radical departure, namely, Pico's essay "On the Dignity of Man," where he holds that man is stationed in the middle of the great chain of being, endowed with freedom either to degenerate to the level of the brute or to ascend and "be reborn into the higher forms which are divine." Man is so much "the maker and moulder of himself that he may fashion himself into whatever shape he shall prefer." The summit of the ascent is an illumination and intoxication whereby man is united with divinity. "Roused by an ineffable love, full of divine power, we shall no longer be ourselves but shall become He Himself who made us."[9] The end is thus deification.

This passage has been characterized as Promethean, but that emphatically it is not. The myth of Prometheus is the picture of man in defiance of the gods inventing and disseminating technological arts. Such a picture one can indeed find in the period of the Renaissance. One has it in a little fantasy of Erasmus, who, finding Colet and some of his friends somewhat heated over a discussion of the nature of the sin of Cain, undertook to relate a diverting story which he professed to have found in some ancient author. In this version, Cain with guile approached the angel with the flaming sword guarding the gate of Paradise in order to wheedle and needle him into passing out some of the luxuriant seeds of Eden. What would God care? inquired Cain. He had forbidden only the apples on one tree. Besides, did the guardian relish his task? From an

[8] Summa Theol. I, 45, 8.

[9] Translated in *The Renaissance Philosophy of Man*, edited by E. Cassirer, P. O. Kristeller and J. H. Randall, 1948 (Phoenix paperback edition now available), p. 225 f.

angel God had made him into an executioner performing the
duty assigned on earth to dogs. To keep men out of Paradise
the sentinel must himself forgo the delights alike of Paradise
and earth, and earth is wondrous fair with vast oceans, lofty
mountains, secluded vales, rivulets leaping down rocky declivi-
ties. There are thousands of trees with lush foliage and perennial fruits. Man is indeed plagued by disease, but there is
nothing which ingenuity and industry cannot surmount. Why
then should the angel brandish his sword against the wind
and deprive himself of such charms, and why should he deprive those who already have so many of a few paltry seeds?
The angel is seduced and Cain achieves such an abundant
yield that God is jealous and plagues him with ants, weevils,
toads, caterpillars, mice, locusts, swine, hail and tornado, and
Cain's propitiatory offering is rejected.[10] This is Promethean
and perhaps it is no accident that it should have been
penned by one trained among the Brethren of the Common
Life, with their insistence on man's ability to imitate the Re-
deemer. Yet, again, how seriously did Erasmus intend his *jeu
d'esprit*, which he related apologetically and with his Mona
Lisa smile?

At any rate, Pico's picture is not this. Technological progress is not his aim, and the displeasure of God is not incurred.
The point is, rather, that man, situated between the beasts and
the angels, has it within his power to descend or to ascend
until he be actually united with God. This is nothing other
than Neoplatonic mysticism, and it is not alien to the Christian tradition into which it had already been incorporated. The
early Greek theologians had declared that God became man
in order that man by union in the Eucharist with God might
become God. For a parallel to Pico's "Dignity of Man" one
may turn to Bonaventura's "Itinerary of the Soul to God,"
where he asserts that although man can do nothing without
divine assistance, he is endowed with faculties enabling him to
cooperate with God. Let man then bestir himself, open his

[10] Ep. 116.

eyes, unstop his ears, that rising above the terrestrial to the celestial he may be wholly transferred and transformed into God. Not without reason does Bonaventura cite Dionysius the Areopagite, that favorite transmitter of the Neoplatonic tradition to the Christian West.

Take another example from the age of the Renaissance, the whimsical fantasy of Giambattista Gelli, who conceived a diverting variant of the story of Ulysses and Circe. In the new version Ulysses prevails upon Circe to restore to human form and to permit to return to their native land all of the Greeks upon her island whom she had transformed into beasts. Circe consents with, however, one stipulation. The Greeks must desire to be restored. Ulysses conveys to them one after another the good news, only to be rebuffed. "For what is man," he is asked, "if not a featherless, hideless biped with no roof upon his back like a turtle or a snail? He must till and toil, whereas nature provides for the animals. Consider, moreover, the diseases to which men are a prey." The serpent, formerly the famous physician Agesimos of Lesbos, is of no mind to return, because the animals do not get sick, and besides physicians know nothing anyway. "How then did you acquire your reputation?" inquires Ulysses, and the candid answer is "By fraud." Men are distraught by fears, racked by passions, and addicted to cruelties. The goat says of his present situation, "*Io sono contento.*" And the deer is not inclined to return, for she had been the wife of a philosopher who insisted that she talk philosophy, in which men are peculiarly adept. Besides when the children are a bawling nuisance they are left to their mothers, and when they become interesting their fathers take over. Nine of the animals declined. Only the elephant, formerly a philosopher, was willing to listen to the praises of man, who by contemplating the beauty of the heavens may change from the terrestrial to the celestial, and casting off the impediments of the flesh—this is addressed to the elephant—may himself become as it were a god. The elephant is at length so enraptured that he bursts into a hymn whose quality can best be appraised if it be given in the original.

> Io canto la prima Cagione di tutte le Cose corruttibili e
>   incorruttibili;
> Quella la quale ha ponderato la terra nel mezzo di questi
>   Cieli;
> Quella la quale ha sparso sopra di lei le acque dolci per
>   alimento de' mortali;
> Quella la quale ha ordinato varie specie di creature per ser-
>   vizio de l'uomo;
> Quella che gli ha dato lo intellette perché egli abbia cogni-
>   zion di lei, e la volontà perché egli possa amarla:
> O forze mie, laudate quella meco.
> Accordatevi con la letizia de l'animo mio, rallegrandovi
>   meco nel gaudio de la mente mia.
> O dote de l'anima mia, cantate meco devotamente la prima
>   ed universal Cagione di tutte le cagioni.
> Accordatevi insieme, lume de lo intelletto mio e libertà
>   de la volonta mia, a cantare le lodi sue.
> L'uomo, animale tuo, o Motore eterno senza fine e senza
>   principio, e quello il quale canta oggi le lodi tue;
> E con tutte le forze sue desidera che a te sia sempre gloria
>   e onore.

> I sing the first cause of all things corruptible and incor-
>   ruptible,
> Who hath weighed the earth in the midst of the heavens,
> And let fall gentle waters for the nutriment of mortals,
> Who hath ordained various kinds of creatures for the
>   services of man,
> Who hath endowed man with intellect to know him and
>   with will to love him;
> May all that is within me bless his name.
> All ye gifts of my soul sing with me the first cause of all
>   causes.
> Join with me, light of my mind and freedom of my will,
> O eternal mover without end and without beginning,

It is today man who sings thy praises,
And with all his powers desires that to thee be given glory
    and honor.[11]

Now what shall be said of this rhapsody? Particularly in the
original it calls to mind, first of all, St. Francis' "Song of
the Creatures." There are besides certain reminiscences of the
Psalms plus a few Aristotelian phrases already incorporated
into the synthesis of Thomas Aquinas. And the whole once
more is suffused with the mysticism of the Florentine Platonic Academy.

A third example serves further to reinforce the point. It
is a prayer placed by Castiglione in the mouth of Bembo and
based upon certain passages in his authentic works.

> Deign, then, O Lord, to hear our prayers, pour thyself
> upon our hearts, and with the splendour of thy most holy
> fire illumine our darkness and, like a trusted guide, in
> this blind labyrinth show us the true path. Correct the
> falseness of our senses, and after our long pursuit of van-
> ities give us true and solid good; make us to inhale those
> spiritual odours that quicken the powers of the intellect,
> and to hear the celestial harmony with such accord that
> there may no longer be room in us for any discord of pas-
> sion; fill us at that inexhaustible fountain of content which
> ever delights and never satiates, and gives a taste of true
> beatitude to all who drink its living and limpid waters;
> with the beams of thy light purge our eyes of misty ignor-
> ance, to the end that they may no longer prize mortal
> beauty, and may know that the things which first they
> seemed to see, are not, and that those which they saw not,
> really are.
>
> Accept our souls, which are offered thee in sacrifice;
> burn them in that living flame which consumes all mortal
> dross, to the end that, being wholly separated from the
> body, they may unite with divine beauty by a perpetual

[11] Giambattista Gelli, *La Circe* (1548), ed. Severino Ferrari (1897),
pp. 139-41.

and very sweet bond, and that we, being severed from ourselves, may, like true lovers, be able to transform ourselves into the beloved, and rising above the earth may be admitted to the angels' feast, where, fed on ambrosia and immortal nectar, we may at last die a most happy and living death, as died of old those ancient fathers whose souls thou, by the most glowing power of contemplation, didst ravish from the body and unite with God."[12]

In this prayer of Bembo, Bonaventura would have missed one Christian essential, and that is a reference to the name of Christ. The same observation applies, of course, to the other two examples. For the Christian mystic, Christ is the mediator, and only by feeding on Him can one taste of God. In these Renaissance writers the Christian note is muted, though never definitely denied, and the door is thereby opened to pass from Christianity, not to irreligion but rather to universal religion.

This becomes the more evident if one turns from the Renaissance view of man to the Renaissance view of God. Immanentism was the kernel of the concept. Now this, of course, is not definitely anti-Christian, and texts in the New Testament were not inappropriately found by way of support. Did not the Apostle Paul say of God, "In Him we live and move and have our being"?[13] Observe, however, that the apostle was quoting a classical poet. Another favorite text was the reference in the Johannine prologue to the immanent light, that "light that lighteth every man that cometh into the world,"[14] because this was interpreted in terms of the Neo-

[12] Translated in H. H. Blanchard, *Prose and Poetry of the Continental Renaissance* (1949), p. 380. On the subject of the dignity of man in the Renaissance compare: Eugenio Garin, "La 'Dignitas hominis' e la Letteratura Patristica," *Rinascita* 1 (1938), pp. 102-46; Herschel Baker, *The Dignity of Man* (1947; Harper Torchbook edition, 1961, under the title, *The Image of Man*).

[13] Acts 17, 28.

[14] John 1, 9.

platonic doctrine of light conceived through metaphysics rather than physics. Light was held to be a form which has to be united with all matter if it is to be capable of visibility. If God is identified with light and if Christ is the light of the world, then God and Christ themselves permeate all reality. In science this meant a vitalistic view of nature, everywhere vibrant, tingling, surging with the energy of God.

Such a view of God, though recurrently appropriated by Christians, is essentially at variance with the main tradition derived from Judaism. Indeed, the Renaissance may be viewed as another of the perennial upsurges of the Hellenic against the Hebraic spirit. For Judaism, God is the transcendent Lord, who from Mount Sinai delivers his commandments to Moses. If this God is brought down from the Mount and made to dwell in every stream and blade, then man finds it easier to discover God everywhere, and the necessity for a unique revelation is less acutely felt. A basis is then discovered for the blending of all religions and the tolerance of all cults.

This process was facilitated in several ways. One was to discover confirmation of Christian doctrines in other religions. The Florentine Academy, for example, discovered in all systems traces and confirmations of the doctrine of Trinity, whether in Plotinus or in the occult lore of the East: the Zoroastrian Oracles, the Hermetic literature, and the Jewish cabala, in which strands of Pythagorean numerical speculation afforded a presumed vindication of the Christian doctrine. So Pico and so Reuchlin in his *De Verbo Mirifico*. Much of the borrowing from classical mythology aspired to be no more than a restating in a new set of symbols of the traditional affirmations.

The second method was the reverse, namely, to purge Christianity of those elements which could not be found in other religions. Servetus, for example, being a Spaniard, was deeply concerned for the problem of the conversion of the Moors and the Jews. To him it appeared that the sole obstacle was the Christian claim that God is both three and one. What then was his relief when, on examining the Scriptures, he could find no mention of the word trinity nor of the related formula of the one substance and the three persons, nor of the key word *homoöusios!* He jettisoned the doctrine in the high hope that unity of religion might thereby be facilitated.

The same general objective was achieved, perhaps unwittingly, by those who, averse to speculation, sought to reduce Christian doctrine to the simplest affirmations. A non-dogmatic piety had characterized the Brethren of the Common Life and their disciple Erasmus, whose patron saint was the penitent thief, since saved with so little theology. This only he believed: that Christ could get him to Paradise. All other beliefs, therefore, are non-essential for salvation. The outcome of such an approach was to reduce Christianity largely to ethics, a blend of Stoicism and the Sermon on the Mount. Little wonder that when in the Enlightenment this position became dominant a similarity was discovered between Christianity and Confucianism!

Still a third way of fostering the concord of all religions was to divest Christianity of its historical core and, by allegory, to impose upon all religions identical meanings. This device was congenial to the mystics who held that religion involved a beginning from within rather than a point of departure from some event without. Such a view negates the essential character of Christianity, resting upon what God did in the fifteenth year of Tiberius. The affirmation that at a point in time God became flesh, suffered, died, and rose, became simply a symbol of the birth of Christ in the soul of man, the dying to sin, and the rising to newness of life. Such was the view of Sebastian Franck. Tolerance for all religions was an inescapable corollary. Highly congenial to such a position was Boccaccio's story of the three identical rings bestowed by a father upon three sons each of whom supposed his ring to be unique. On the father's death the three proved to be indistinguishable. Now, these are Christianity, Judaism, and Islam.[15]

Our next inquiry is to ask what bearing these developments had upon the church, and the answer is that there was very little overt clash between the exponents of the positions delineated above and the Church of Rome. If the advocates of the New Learning suffered at the hands of the Church, it was only in the second half of the sixteenth century, during the period of the Counter-Reformation. In the heyday of the Renaissance Pico was merely looked upon askance, whereas the thoroughly medieval Savonarola went to the gallows. The reason was partly that the popes were themselves the patrons of the new learning and the new art, and they were not passionately concerned about religion. Moreover, the humanists lacked the temper of martyrs. They were ready to go just up to the edge of the fire, since to die for an idea is to put too high a price upon a conjecture.

Skepticism was not rife, and such as we do find is to be understood rather as a heritage from the Middle Ages than as a new development of the age of the Renaissance. It consisted in a dualism between philosophy and theology, two disciplines capable of arriving at contradictory conclusions. Two Christian doctrines were in this way called into question. The first was personal immortality and the second was the doctrine of the Trinity. The difficulty with regard to immortality stemmed from the Arabic influence, for the Arabs interpreted Aristotle as meaning that at death the individual soul is absorbed into the world soul. The energy is not lost, but the identity is submerged. In our period, Pomponazzi stood in this tradition and in his work on immortality endeavored to demonstrate by a more acute examination of the mind-body problem that no evidence and no analogy point to continuance of personal

---

[15] Jacob Burckhardt, *The Civilization of the Renaissance in Italy* (Harper Torchbook edition, 1958), p. 475, asserts that the story of the three rings, though much older than Boccaccio, is first used by him to place Christianity on a par with the other religions (Decam. 1, Nov. 3).

consciousness after the dissolution of the body. One may wonder why no action was taken against Pomponazzi, and the answer is that he was perfectly covered by the doctrine of double truth, or at least of double logic, which held that philosophy and theology, far from being related as maid and mistress, are divergent and often contradictory quests for truth. What is philosophically indefensible may be theologically sound. Pomponazzi was quite prepared, therefore, to believe in personal immortality, although he could not bolster his conviction by physiological or philosophical underpinning.

A similar position arose out of late scholasticism which called itself Modernism. This view made difficulty for the doctrine of the Trinity, that God is both three and one, because these philosophers took an atomistic view of reality, which, according to them, is made up of individual components which are not held together by any comprehensive entities. The State, for example, cannot be regarded as a corporate entity but only as an agglomeration of citizens. Likewise, the Church. If this theory be applied to the three persons in God, that is to say, if they cannot be held in unity by the entity of the one substance, then there must be three gods. The doctrine of the Trinity becomes thereby the doctrine of tritheism. But once again, tritheism was not affirmed, because theology rules otherwise. Here, likewise, one kind of logic compels the conclusion that there are three gods, whereas another points to monotheism. The decision rests with the Church. When, however, the authority of the Church was undercut by the Protestant Reformation, then Servetus employed all of these late scholastic arguments to reinforce his objection to the doctrine of the Trinity.

Beyond this there was little skepticism. But one or two examples of a somewhat flippant criticism of Biblical miracles can be discovered in the same number of centuries. Luigi Pulci suggested that Moses might have unloosed the floodgates of a fishpond and drowned a few of Pharoah's men, that Samson carried off the door of a summer booth, and that

Peter walked on a frozen sea.[16] Indirect ridicule was poked
at Joshua's exploit by relating that Charlemagne for three
days stopped the sun in order to complete a victory, and
thereby gravely inconvenienced the people on the other side
of the earth. Pietro d'Abano, as early as 1300, is credited
with a rationalistic explanation of the resurrection of Lazarus.
But serious skepticism is scarcely discoverable prior to the
very end of the sixteenth century when Bruno, Campanella,
and Vanni expiated their temerity at the stake after the manner of the high Middle Ages.[17]

Satire and ridicule of the Church were common enough.
Although serious in intent, they were not revolutionary in
objective. The authors were minded to correct abuses but not
to destroy the structure of the Church. Witness the Pasqui-
nades and Facetiae. Take, for example, the anecdote related
by Poggio Bracciolini that a certain priest buried his pet dog
in consecrated ground. The bishop remonstrated. The priest
explained, "Father, if you knew the cunning of this dog, his
intelligence was more than human in his lifetime, and especially manifest at his death, for he made a will and, knowing that you were needy, left you fifty golden ducats. Here
they are." The dog was undisturbed. The relater of this
tale was a papal secretary and he also was undisturbed.[18]

More subversive to the church was the literary criticism of
documents and the exposure of forgeries undertaken by
Lorenzo Valla. He demonstrated that the Donation of Constantine, which claimed that this emperor had conferred upon
the pope temporal sovereignty over the whole of the West,
could not have arisen in the days of Constantine, because of
variations in the Latin and certain historical allusions which
necessitated a date not much in advance of the time of Charle-

[16] Ernst Walser, "Die Religion des Luigi Pulci," *Die neueren
Sprachen*, Beiheft X (1926).

[17] G. Spini, *Ricerca dei Libertini* (1950).

[18] In translation in Merrick Whitcomb, *A Literary Source Book of the
Italian Renaissance* (1900), p. 35.

magne. The Apostles' Creed was shown by Valla not to have originated with the Apostles. Likewise, the letter of Christ to Abgar of Edessa was proved not to have been genuine. On this letter rested an elaborate superstructure. In the letter Christ promised to send Abgar his portrait. So many portraits came to be extant, each claiming to be genuine, that the church selected one as the true image, the Veron-Ikon, whence the name Veronica, and the legend of her napkin. Valla likewise wrote critical notes on the New Testament text which, after his death, were published by Erasmus. Yet Valla held a post as papal secretary. The Church was sufficiently entrenched that the loss of a few documents did not unsettle her foundations.

Only one serious clash occurred between the humanists and the Church. It was the Reuchlin affair and had to deal with freedom to pursue Semitic studies. Reuchlin, a layman, was invited to give a judgment because a converted Jew named Pfefferkorn was displaying the zeal of a convert in clamoring for the destruction of Jewish books. Reuchlin, who believed that the Jewish cabala offered a confirmation of the doctrine of the Trinity, rallied to the defense. The upshot of the affair was a tacit victory for the humanists. Reuchlin was indeed saddled with the costs of the trial, but he never paid them, and Semitic studies went valiantly on. Was it not Cardinal Ximenes who published the Complutensian Polyglot containing the Hebrew text of the Old Testament?

The Renaissance then was rather subversive by the subtle transmutation of values noted above: syncretism, allegorization, moralization, the reduction of dogma, the spiritualizing of everything external. These exercised a corrosive influence so imperceptibly that none took fright until the Reformation commenced the exposure of the Renaissance and then the Counter-Reformation turned upon them both.

By way of gathering up the themes, we may inquire as to the mood of the Renaissance. Commonly, it is represented as exuberant, unconcerned, blithe, without twinges of conscience, pangs of remorse, or tremors of anxiety. Again, there is some measure of truth in this generalization, but the change in tone from the Middle Ages can easily be overdone. The exuberance of the Renaissance is not to be exaggerated. There was at the same time a strain of melancholy, and Petrarch suffered from *accidie*,[19] the typical monkish slough of despond, a doubt not only as to the vocation but with regard to the central affirmations of the faith. Renaissance man was not so sure of his knowledge. Nicolaus of Cusa pushed to the upper limits the reach of the human understanding and eventuated in learned ignorance, *docta ignorantia*. Agrippa of Nettesheim wrote on "The Uncertainty of All the Sciences" (*De Incertitudine Omnium Scientarium*). Some even made a virtue of necessity and acquiesced in ignorance on the ground that knowledge puffed one up. A *docta ignorantia* was matched by a *sacra ignorantia*.

Neither did Renaissance man feel so certain that he was the master of his fate. Pico held that man was the moulder of his destiny and could descend and ascend in the scale of being, because Pico did not believe in astrology; but many did. And one of the great problems of the Renaissance was whether *Virtu* was able to impede the wheels of the goddess Fortuna.

Expressions of despondency are not uncommon. Erasmus indulged in wistful scoffing at the very endeavors to which he had consecrated the unremitting toil of a lifetime. "Why inflict upon oneself," he inquired, "invalidism, sore eyes, and premature age in the making of books, when per chance wisdom lies with babes?" Dürer, in his *Melencolia* poignantly displays the plight of man, the exuberant, confronted by the unresolved decisions of destiny. A woman of high intelligence broods torpidly amid all the symbols of man's highest skills. Only the little cherub scribbling at her side is insouciant of the forces at play—for in the sky a rainbow, the sign of God's covenant with man, contains a comet, the symbol of impend-

[19] Giulio A. Levi, "Accidia e Dubbio nel Petrarca," *Rinascita* I (1938), pp. 40-47.

ing disaster. Until the conflict in the heavenly places be resolved, what is the meaning of man's endeavor?

Where did man turn for solace? Erasmus looked to traditional Catholic Christianity. He is sometimes regarded as religiously shallow because he wrote only in a foreign tongue. This was true perhaps until the final hour. As he lay dying he murmured, first in Latin, *Miserere mihi,* and then in Dutch, *Liefe Godt.* Dürer found his resolution in the rediscovery of the gospel by Martin Luther, the man who had released him from great anguish of spirit. Michelangelo, in accord with the forms of traditional medieval piety, took his stand at the foot of the Cross.

> Freed from a burden sore and grievous bond,
>> Dear Lord, and from this wearying world untied,
>> Like a frail bark I turn me to Thy side,
>> As from a fierce storm to a tranquil land.
> Thy thorns, Thy nails and either bleeding hand,
>> With Thy mild gentle piteous face, provide
>> Promise of help and mercies multiplied,
>> And hope that yet my soul secure may stand.
> Let not Thy holy eyes be just to see
>> My evil past, Thy chastened ears to hear
>> And stretch the arm of judgment to my crime:
> Let Thy blood only lave and succour me,
>> Yielding more perfect pardon, better cheer,
>> As older still I grow with lengthening time.[20]

If then the Renaissance was so near to the kingdom of God, why the conflict with the Reformation? Here it is striking to observe that the most intense clash occurred not with the least but with the most Christian representatives of the Renaissance. Luther attacked not the ribald Aretino or the trifling Boccaccio, but, rather, the great restorer of primitive Christianity, Erasmus of Rotterdam. And Calvin came to grips not

---

[20] Translated by J. A. Symonds, *The Sonnets of Michel Angelo Buonarroti* (1902).

with the scoffing Luigi Pulci, but with the passionate herald of the new day of the Lord, Michael Servetus.

The reason was that the Reformation marked a return to the Judaic element in Christianity, to the concept of God as high and lifted up, who is known to man not because He is everywhere obviously immanent, but because, normally veiled in obscurity, He has, in a point of time, disclosed Himself in Jesus Christ, and in Him enacted a great drama of redemption upon Calvary, only by believing in which—and not by beginning from within—can man be saved. No moral achievement can ever give any claim upon God, and no ascending of the ladder of the chain of being can ever unite man with God and make him into God. The very notion of the deification of humanity was to Calvin blasphemous. Man, who is no clod or clay or lump—he has, in fact, all the excellent qualities which the humanists attributed to him—is nevertheless dust and ashes before God the All-High and the All-Holy. Not by achievement but by trust is man saved, and morality itself is only the by-product of religion, the behavior springing from gratitude to God for his unspeakable gifts.

If the Renaissance be defined as a movement which can be set over against the Reformation, then the Renaissance was marked mainly by an exaggeration of the Hellenic elements in the Christian synthesis, with an ever-present tendency to destroy the distinctiveness of the Christian revelation. And in some quarters there was a secularistic tendency which relegated religion to the periphery of life. But if the Renaissance be defined as a chronological period which includes the Reformation, then one may say that, although the unity of the Church was shattered, the Christian consciousness of Europe was restored.

V FROM PETRARCH
TO SHAKESPEARE

by Leicester Bradner

I am very grateful to my colleagues on this symposium for their discussion on the date boundaries of the Renaissance, for it has been apparent that this is a problem causing some confusion and misunderstanding. In dealing with literature I am obliged to beg indulgence for using the widest possible limits. Renaissance literature began in the mid-fourteenth century in Italy, yet in other countries a medieval type of writing prevailed until the end of the fifteenth century, and one cannot talk about Shakespeare and Cervantes without overlapping slightly into the seventeenth.

The literature of the Renaissance, then, is not easily described. The period itself, as it moves from medieval feudalism towards democratic capitalism and the modern national state, and from the faith of St. Francis toward the rationalism of the eighteenth century, is full of contradictions. It never reached a plateau of stability like the twelfth century or the age of Newton, Pope, and Voltaire. This is equally true of its creative literature. One cannot say that the ironic wit of Ariosto is any more typical of the Renaissance than the beauty and idealism of Spenser, or that the *Arcadia* of Sannazaro is any more representative than the rudely boisterous world of *Gargantua*. When looked at from the point of view of western Europe as a whole, it shows a diversity which almost defies generalization.

I am full of admiration at the various ways in which my predecessors have simplified the complicated problems presented by their subject matter. Mr. Sarton particularly pleased me with his comparison of the history of science to a series of twelve panel paintings. I confess that I have not been able to

achieve a similar simplification for literature. Instead of a series
of neat panels I am obliged to offer a great crowded wall-
painting—one of those fields full of folk which Mark Twain
referred to as ten-acre pictures—a landscape full of bays and
mountains, with rivers winding here and there and groups of
figures going hither and thither about their business without
any apparent relation to each other. My task will be to try to
guide you through this maze so that, when you finally reach
that peak which you see there way off in the left-hand background, you may be able to look back and observe the path
by which you came. At various places on this picture map you
will see scrolls bearing the names of countries. Here in the
foreground is the legend ITALIA, in the center is FRANCIA, off
to the left we read HISPANIA, and in the distance, just beyond
that small body of water, is the word ANGLIA, written a little
larger than the others because the compiler of this map was
a professor of English literature.

The story of Renaissance literature is the story of Italian
literature and its influence upon these other countries: how
they reacted to it, where they followed it, and, even more significant, where they did not follow it. In pursuing this line of
approach, generalizations about the revival of the classics, the
rise of secularism, the rise of the new national spirit, and the
new conception of romantic love will find their places as we
go along.

France had dominated medieval literature. Its great poetry
had been the expression of an aristocratic courtly spirit flourishing in the castles of the great feudal lords. The literature
which it produced in the twelfth and thirteenth centuries was
as great and varied as any that the world has given us, but it
stopped just short of the most outstanding figures. There were
no Vergils, no Dantes, no Shakespeares. By the fourteenth
century, it was in a slow decay which lasted until the time of
Marot and Rabelais.

Italy now entered the picture with the creative vigor of its
prosperous growing towns. Dante, although his material is

medieval, is an outstanding example of this new spirit; and close on his heels come Petrarch and Boccaccio, whose material marks a sharp break with the medieval tradition. And with Petrarch and Boccaccio the new enthusiasm for the classics appears.

The recovery and mental digestion of the classics occupied Italian intellectuals during the fifteenth century. Vernacular literature stood still while men learned the lessons of form and style taught by the great ancient writers. They learned how to be brief and pointed in the epigram and the Horatian ode as well as in their own late-medieval form, the sonnet. They learned that a comedy or a tragedy must have clear-cut form if it is to be dramatically effective, and they learned that an epic should be written according to a definite plan. And all of these things they learned mostly by writing in the Latin language.

Then came the outburst of creation in the vernacular, led by the courts of Florence and Naples, but soon finding even greater expression in the writers patronized by the Este family in Ferrara. This new vernacular Italian literature was aristocratic and courtly in its origin, just as French medieval literature had been, but the Italian courts were not isolated from the new bourgeois culture of the towns; rather, they were the expression of it. The Medici were not ancient royalty; they were bankers who had taken over the Florentine state. When Pulci, who wrote for the Medici, deals with the heroes of the Charlemagne cycle they become sensible men of the world and engage in many humorous activities—such as cultivating the acquaintance of two rather vulgar and amusing giants.

When comedies are written for court production they are imitations of the middle class comedies of Plautus. Only in tragedy is the old high line of kings and great personages adhered to. And the short stories, the *novelle*, were just the things, in both length and subject matter, to amuse the tired businessman. They would hardly have amused the twelfth century audience of Chrétien de Troyes, or even that of Jean de Meung. But one must not push this point too far. Such a medieval audience would not have felt strange in the woman-worshipping world of Petrarch's sonnets, nor in the sentimental beauty of Sannazaro's *Arcadia*.

To such an extent was this new Italian literature the basis for the literature of the other countries that we must stop to describe it more fully. The first point to be made is that it was characterized by great formal excellence in both structure and style. Alone among European countries, Italy had established a mature vernacular style in the fourteenth century which has lasted through to the present day without any important language changes to disrupt it. In England the change from Middle English to Modern English made the style of Chaucer and Langland impossible after 1500, and much the same thing happened in France.

The Italians, however, by combining the examples of their own writers with those of the newly-read classics, were able to produce, around the year 1500, works in both prose and verse, whose force and elegance were the admiration of Europe. Petrarch had already provided a complete vocabulary for the dissection of melancholy love in poetry, and now Sannazaro, drawing heavily upon Vergil's *Eclogues*, did the same for prose. What was desirable in literature was also desirable in sophisticated social life. Castiglione, in his dialogues entitled *The Courtier*, raised conversational style to a high level and inspired countless imitators in all other countries. And in the expression of wit and irony Ariosto, both in his brilliant comedies and in his *Orlando Furioso*, left little to be desired. It remained to be shown that eloquence could, when necessary, be disciplined and pruned to serious practical use. With Machiavelli's *Prince*, Italy again took the lead.

Structure was a lesson which the new literature needed to learn even more than style. Rambling was the characteristic fault of the late medieval writers. The dream visions, so popular in their time, induced a kind of sleeping sickness which was fatal to clarity of form. Here, then, is the great service performed by the humanists with their sometimes heavy-handed idolatry of the classics. They did insist upon form. A play must be in five acts and must follow certain rules of plot structure. An epic must begin in the middle, must contain supernatural motivation, and must end in the hero's victory. A pastoral eclogue must be a conversation between two shepherds and must end neatly with the driving home of the flocks or with the award of a prize. In prose, the dialogue form is the best way to present an argument.

What this contribution meant may be illustrated by comparing the comedies of Ariosto and Machiavelli with the crude horseplay of the English moralities or of the French farce at the beginning of the sixteenth century; or one may compare Corraro's finely wrought, if imitative, tragedy of *Progne,* which the Oxford dons had the good taste to produce for Queen Elizabeth's visit in 1566, with the incredibly primitive and vulgarized tragedy of *Orestes,* written in England during the same decade.

The Italians not only provided distinguished models of good literary form by their activity within the traditional branches of literature; they also created two new forms which were very influential in European literature. These were the pastoral romance and the romantic epic.

The pastoral romance may owe some vague debt to the late classical *Daphnis and Chloe,* but in most respects it is a new creation by Boccaccio in the *Ameto.* This was neglected by the fifteenth century until Sannazaro revived the form in his more famous *Arcadia.* Here the supposed shepherds are really sophisticated aristocrats, who discuss their love affairs with a gently elegant melancholy punctuated by bursts of Petrarchan poetry. Out of this grew Montemayor's *Diana* in Spain, Sidney's *Arcadia* in England, and the French romances of the seventeenth century.

The romantic epic, one of Italy's greatest contributions to Renaissance literature, arose in the courts of Florence and

Ferrara to fill the gap caused by the gradual decay and falling out of favor of the great medieval romances of the Charlemagne and Arthur cycles. The poets who wrote them, Pulci, Boiardo, and Ariosto, knew Vergil and the classical rules, but consciously elected to deal with popular material in a popular way. Here only was there a refusal to follow the classics in the Italian Renaissance. Ariosto, to jump immediately to the greatest of the three, showed such skill and variety of mood in the episodic narratives of the *Orlando Furioso* that he surpassed in poetry the short stories of the *Decameron*. Crisscrossing his multiple plots with bewildering frequency, he nevertheless made each incident a gem of sophisticated entertainment at one time or of delicate pathos at another, so that the reader is constantly led on in search of new treasure. His wit and irony, his mature technique, far outdid anything yet produced in Italy, and his poem became both a model of style and a storehouse of plots for all the other countries in Europe.

The foregoing summary gives rise to one rather curious conclusion, namely, that Italian literature of this period was remarkably successful in two seemingly opposite ways. In the sentimentality and concern with personal feelings in Petrarch and Sannazaro, an elaborate technique was developed for dealing with manners and sentiments. Carried into the courtly sphere, this same technique is exemplified by the eloquent and sophisticated discussions of the characters in the works of Bembo and Castiglione. But, on the other hand, Italians were equally successful in the field of hardheaded realism: the cynical intrigue plots of the *novelle*, the comedy of deception on the Italian stage, and the cold-blooded dissection of motives in Machiavelli's *Prince*.

Finally, we may remark that the Italians were the storytellers *par excellence* for all of Europe. English, French, and Spanish drama were indebted to them for hundreds of plots— the example of Shakespeare will occur to everyone—and the sonnet situations from Petrarch were used over and over again. When Spenser wanted materials for his tremendously long narrative poem, *The Faerie Queene*, it was from the Italians again that he got most of his incidents.

Yet, with all this profusion of story material, there is a strange lack of feeling for character. Not one of the great characters of Renaissance literature is from the Italian. Think of Gargantua, Don Quixote, Don Juan, Doctor Faustus, Hamlet, Falstaff, Volpone, Sir Epicure Mammon—and then try to think of any one from Italian literature to match them. Certainly, Ariosto's Angelica is not a match for the heroines of Shakespeare or Cervantes. Even Boccaccio's Criseide is far inferior to Chaucer's. Perhaps the nearest to a great individual character from Italy is Pulci's humorous giant, Morgante.

A word should be added about Italian criticism. From their early study of the classical writers the Italian critics took the lead chronologically; and their vigorous pronouncements on literary problems of all kinds, especially those on the nature of epic and drama, formed the basis on which the literary criticism of all other countries was built.

When the impulse toward new literary expression moved northward and westward from Italy, some important changes took place, particularly in England and Spain. France, although it produced great original writers in Rabelais, D'Aubigné, and Montaigne, did so more by going outside the range of Italian literature than by making changes in the Italian forms. In Germany there was no creative literature of importance at this time. France, England, and Spain all followed the lead of Italy in the beginning, but all, to one degree or another, asserted their independence and ended by producing something quite different. In England, especially, medieval literary precedents were very powerful and refused to be overwhelmed by outside influences, whether classical or Italian.

The Italian form which preserved itself most successfully in other countries was the sonnet sequence. The great exemplar, Petrarch, came very early, and there were many Italian imitators before any foreigners came into the field.

These native imitators all fall far short of their master in the creation of a complete sequence, no matter how powerful some of their individual sonnets may be. It would almost seem as if Petrarch had so completely stamped the sequence with his own personality and methods that no one else could do other than weakly copy him. His personal lack of success in his suit to Laura and her subsequent death gave a melancholy tinge to all later sequences and established the sonnet lady once and for all as unyielding to the lover's passion. Thus, the descriptions of the lady's beauty, the statements of undying devotion, the complaints of the torments of love soon became standardized in the sonnet writers of all countries. Very few have the dramatic power of Sidney's *Astrophel and Stella,* the white-hot passion of Shakespeare's Dark Lady sonnets, or the autumnal charm of Ronsard's sonnets to Hélène. Even though these great writers do succeed in giving a personal stamp to a product which had become subject to all the defects of mass production, they rarely depart in any striking way from the Petrachan model. When we do find a writer like Du Bellay, who writes a non-Petrarchan sequence, we see that, although the poems are all sonnets, the subject matter is that of a collection of epigrams. The sonnet sequence is the Italian form least changed in transit.

It was largely through the sonnets and the other lyrical poems of the Italians that Neoplatonism was spread throughout Europe. Starting with Ficino's theory of the place of beauty and love in the progress of the soul towards God, the idealistic elements in this philosophy spread, often in a vague and diffused form, all over Europe. Whether used vaguely or specifically, they form an important contribution of Italian thought in many poets of the Renaissance. Passing into prose literature in the famous speech of Bembo in the fourth book of Castiglione's *Courtier,* they were also spread by the immense popularity of that work.

When we turn from the sonnet to the pastoral romance a different situation meets us. Sannazaro, building on Boccaccio's

Ameto, produced the great Renaissance archetype, the *Arcadia.* Though written in prose it has many interpolated verses and is essentially the work of a poet who is combining Vergil with Petrarch. The characters, who are anything but real shepherds, move around in an atmosphere of elegant melancholy and rather vaguely discuss their unsuccessful love affairs. Its popularity was a triumph of style and of mood. The *Arcadia,* however, had neither plot nor action enough to satisfy the spirit of vigorous rising nationalism operating in the minds of Spaniards and Englishmen. When the Spaniard Montemayor took over the pastoral romance, fifty years later, he put in real plots—a series of interlocking love triangles—and made his psychological situation more interesting by mixing real country dwellers with exiles from the court who are merely taking a momentary respite from the cares of the world. From the point of view of style and beauty one would perhaps rather read Sannazaro, but for story interest Montemayor was easily superior. The pastoral atmosphere and praise of country life were, however, retained.

Finally, after a lapse of another generation, Sir Philip Sidney undertook to write a pastoral romance. He borrowed from Sannazaro the name Arcadia and the idea of interpolating prose with poetry, but little else. Shepherds to Sidney are either picturesque figures who give rustic entertainments for the upper classes or else they are comic clowns, but they will not do for main characters. Similarly, Sidney is not satisfied with the episodic linked triangle plots of Montemayor; he demands a real organized plot like that of a drama. His two young heroes enter Arcadian life in disguise only because they have fallen in love with the daughters of a foolish old king who has retired to the country in fear of an oracle. From this point the plot proceeds quite realistically to deal with their adventures in winning the princesses and restoring the king to his capital. Sidney was not satisfied, as Sannazaro was, with the ideal of retirement from the world. He introduced heroic action, questions of state policy, examples of good and bad rulers. In other words, matters which Renaissance criticism regarded as proper to the epic have been introduced into and allowed to dominate a form which started out in Italy as poetic literature of escape. Yet without the *Arcadia* of Sannazaro there would not have been the *Arcadia* of Sidney.

At the opposite extreme from the unreal sentimental fiction of Sannazaro was the realistic fiction of the short stories of Boccaccio and his later imitators, Cinthio and Bandello. Plot and situation were their stock in trade. Character and atmosphere were usually non-existent. They formed, as we have said, a great storehouse of plot material used again and again by all the rest of Europe. They remained, however, separate stories; there was no progress towards what we would call a novel. Here is where Spain made its greatest contribution to Renaissance literature and to the literature of later periods. Beginning with the *Celestina*, a long realistic narrative in dialogue form, written in 1499, the way led on through *Lazarillo de Tormes*, which founded the picaresque school, up to the world masterpiece of Cervantes shortly after 1600. Now, doubtless without the example of the Italian *novelle* there would have been no demand for realistic fiction and no urge to write it, but certainly what the Spanish writers did write was highly original and little indebted to their predecessors. Furthermore, what they wrote was very significant for the future. In *Lazarillo de Tormes*, a much underrated work, we see the world for the first time from the point of view of the needy and dispossessed, from the point of view of those whose sight is sharpened by hunger and necessity. Just as in England, the attack is mainly on the newly rich and the purse-proud. The one master who was loved and respected by Lazarillo was the decayed representative of the true old nobility.

As for *Don Quixote*, we here meet one of the great works of human genius. It is not, of course, an attack on the old romances; it is the story of a man who fell in love with all that was good and noble in them and went out into the world to try to practice it, and the world defeated him. He is something of a hero and something of a saint, but he is treated ironically and realistically. In some ways, he is like Shakespeare's King Lear, but, unlike King Lear, he is not allowed to die in a burst of courage and love. Tragedy for him is not madness but restoration to sanity. The conflicts and uncertainties of the sixteenth century have introduced into literature a new way of writing tragedy, a way which perhaps owes something to the ironic attitude of More and Erasmus, but which had to wait for Cervantes before it could receive the creative myth-making power which could make it immortal and add one more figure to that great society of imagined persons who are so much more memorable than the real persons of history.

One more name must be mentioned in connection with prose fiction, one which does not fit as neatly into the picture as those of the Spaniards. It is, of course, Rabelais. His giants owe something to medieval popular legend and something to the good-natured giants of Pulci, but what he does with them is quite different. Perhaps what we have is a combination of Erasmus and folklore. Here is all the Erasmian attack on monkish ignorance and decayed scholasticism but delivered in great swashing blows and accompanied with roars of belly-laughter. Erasmus uses irony as his method; Rabelais uses—and often very effectively—farce, burlesque, and parody. Erasmus wished to substitute the discipline of the New Testament for the endless maze of superstition and over-elaborated ritual which he thought characterized the church of the time. But Rabelais wanted no discipline at all, except self-discipline. Be natural, he says, and all will be good clean fun. As a writer of fiction he is less important than as a conveyor of ideas. Starting off with a relatively interesting story, he degenerates in his later books into long arguments among his characters. Yet no writer in the Renaissance shows a healthier realism or a more powerful creative urge.

Of all the major literary forms, the one most highly honored in the Renaissance was the epic. Italian critics asserted that it was the highest form and discussed it elaborately. Writers in all countries practiced it. The fame of Vergil's celebration of the Roman Empire made it imperative that the new nationalistic spirit should be expressed in national epics. In Italy, which was not politically organized as a single nation, this was not felt; but since the Italians considered themselves the heirs of the Romans, a Roman theme could fill the bill. So Petrarch composed large portions of an unfinished epic on the defeat of Carthage, and Trissino composed a complete one on the liberation of Italy from the Goths. These were regular epics, that is, they followed the classical rules, illustrated by Vergil, of beginning in the middle, using supernatural powers, and ending with the victory of the hero. Love, again as in Vergil, is introduced but is not made a major element in the poem. But, as we have seen, one of Italy's great contributions to Renaissance literature was the non-classical or romantic epic which reached its peak in the *Orlando Furioso*. In poems of this sort the classics are constantly raided for incidents and for beauties of style, but the narrative method is the straightforward storytelling of the medieval romances. The writers of these epics knew that Vergil, like themselves, had worked under a patronage system, and they saw nothing wrong in adapting their poems to such a system. Ordinarily, the method followed was to introduce a real or mythical ancestor of the patron into the story and make him either the hero or a prominent character. Thus Ruggiero in Ariosto's plot is the ancestor of the dukes of Ferrara; Britomart and Arthegal in *The Faerie Queene* are ancestors of Queen Elizabeth; and in an epic on the conquest of the New World by Giorgini, which is dedicated to the children of Philip II, their great-grandfather Ferdinand is represented, quite unhistorically, as leading the campaign in Mexico.

An interesting and characteristic preference for recent history as epic material is shown by the Spanish poets. Since their own country had been but newly put together by the union of Castile and Aragon and by the conquest of the Moors, they sought to celebrate the deeds of the immediate past rather than those of mythical history. Giorgini, it is true, was an Italian writing for Spanish patrons, but the Spanish poets themselves did the same thing, producing epics on Charles V, on Cortés, and on campaigns in South America. In Portugal this holds true of Camoens' *Lusiads*, which tells the story of Vasco da Gama's great voyage around Africa to the cities of India. All of these poems follow the method and even the stanza form of Ariosto. None of them, except the *Lusiads*, achieved high rank as literature. Just as we see a hardheaded realism in the Spanish fiction we have been discussing, so here we see among these people a tendency to stick to the actual facts of history rather than to use the more malleable material of myth.

In France, where classical standards held stronger sway, the epic did not flourish. Of poems in the tradition of Ariosto, there were none; and when Ronsard, the greatest of French sixteenth-century poets, attempted a regular classic epic on Francus, the mythical founder of France, he was unable to get beyond the fourth book. The fragment was published but is regarded as a failure. Nevertheless, its existence shows the strength of the universal urge towards epics which had been started by the Italians. When D'Aubigné wished to deal with epic materials provided by the heroic resistance of the Huguenots in France, he found himself without a hero, for Henry of Navarre had been reconciled to the Roman Catholic Church in 1593. His poem, *Les Tragiques*, is not an epic—it is not even historical in method—but it deals with historical materials. At times it rises to heights of impassioned eloquence unmatched elsewhere in Renaissance literature. Even in Scotland, a minor poet named Melville started out to write an epic on Gathelus, the mythical founder of his country, of which a fragment is preserved in manuscript.

England offers the most instructive example of the influence of Ariosto and the way in which it merged with other influences. We know that Spenser started out to imitate Ariosto

in *The Faerie Queene;* we know from the poem itself how
unlike Ariosto his work is. Yet the poem is full of material
from the *Orlando Furioso.* There are at least four ways in
which Spenser deals differently with what is essentially the
same kind of material. First, Spenser was not satisfied with
the formlessness of Ariosto's poem. He considered himself a
disciple of Vergil and was pained by the rambling of his
Italian model. Therefore, he made an heroic attempt to impose Vergilian form upon Ariostian materials. Although he
preserved the use of many heroes in one poem, he treated the
main deeds of each hero in a separate book which came to a
definite conclusion. And in an attempt to create some sort of
unity to the whole plot structure, he made the Faerie Queene
herself the object of loyal devotion on the part of all his
heroes and promised that the poem would end with a great
feast at which they would all be present.

But the division into at least partially unified books does not
arise entirely from devotion to Vergil; it arises quite as much
from Spenser's place as a Protestant Englishman in the
tradition of northern humanism with its special emphasis on
Christian ethics, for each book is devoted to the illustration
of a moral or religious virtue. This is the second way in which
Spenser differs radically from his model, and it leads to the
third. Spenser's poem deals with ideas in a way in which
Ariosto's does not and never intends to. Spenser was not a
philosopher, but he liked to think—and, along with Sidney,
he believed—that creative literature should contain plenty
of thought. Not only the moral virtues but such major concepts as love (in the largest sense), mutability, justice, and
international relations are woven into the texture of his
poem, not through disquisitions by his characters after the
manner of Castiglione, but through involving them in the
plot. And in speaking of international relations, I have come
to the last point. Spenser, like the Spaniards, is concerned
about contemporary history, but he deals with it through
symbol and allegory rather than through telling the facts of

history. Mary Queen of Scots, Philip II of Spain, Henry of Navarre, and the Pope are never mentioned in the poem, but they are never very long out of our thoughts.

The Faerie Queene, then, is the most complete example of the process of fusion that went on in the creating of Renaissance literature outside Italy. The impulse, the inspiration, came from Italy, the mythical history of the Arthurian legends came from England, the ethical tone from northern humanism, and the intellectual content from the general Renaissance criticism of the epic which had started in Italy, stating that it should embody ideas and ideals as well as heroic action.

This conflicting and merging of influences is best observed in the drama, where a strong medieval tradition was already in possession of the field when the Renaissance began. All over Europe the rudimentary liturgical plays of the church had developed into popular cycles of Biblical plays which were at their height in the fourteenth and fifteenth centuries, and alongside of these there grew up also the immensely vigorous tradition of the popular morality play. Together these two forms of drama had developed a vigorous acting tradition and a repertoire of themes both comic and tragic, even though in range of subject matter they were as yet severely restricted. Strongly typed characters, too, such as the ranting tyrant, the shrewish wife, the witty servant, and the comic half-wit, had become established as standard figures on the stage. But, on the other hand, there was little sense of structure. With rare exceptions, the Bible story itself was enough for the dramatist, and in the moralities three or four standard situations sufficed for all the plays.

Into the midst of this situation came the new knowledge of the comedies of Plautus and Terence and the tragedies of Seneca, with their act and scene structure and their carefully contrived plots based upon deception, irony, and surprise. The Italian courts took them up with enthusiasm, both for reading and for actual performance. Any writer who wanted a court audience for an original play was obligated to imitate these models, whether he wrote in Latin or Italian. Thus there arose at the end of the fifteenth century in Italy a school of dramatic writers who far exceeded the rest of Europe in purely technical skill, however dreary their content may sometimes have been. But it is a mistake to assume that the content was always dreary. In comedy, the Italians were highly successful imitators of Roman comedy, and Roman comedy is not dull. In the hands of masters like Ariosto and Machiavelli this type of comedy became adapted to contemporary Italian life with brilliant results. Witness its influence upon Ben Jonson a century later. It was a comedy of deception and intrigue, of misers, parasites, gay young men and lost heiresses; it depended on plot rather than character, and the characters it used were highly typed; but it was clever, amusing, and very actable. At its best, in Machiavelli, it could rise to mordant satire upon the evils of society, but in general it was lighthearted amusement.

In tragedy, the Italians never got much beyond frigid correctness. This was in large part the result of their failure to domesticate Latin tragedy to the Italian scene in the way they domesticated Plautus to the streets of Florence and Ferrara. They perversely ransacked classical legend for plots instead of turning to the tragic themes available in their own literature. And when at last, at the very end of the Italian Renaissance, a writer like Giraldi Cinthio began to turn to the *novelle* for tragic plots the result was merely an accumulation of more than Senecan horrors. The characters simply did not seem like real people. It was left for Shakespeare to make effective use of the stories of Romeo and Juliet and Othello and Desdemona, and for Webster to see the real possibilities in the death of the Duchess of Malfi.

Even in the classics themselves, they either pass by or fail to breathe any life into the themes immortalized by Shakespeare and given at least respectable treatment by Ben Jonson. Finally, one may add that their failure in tragedy is connected with their failure to create memorable characters. If a tragedy is to achieve high rank it must convince us that the character whose fall is depicted had elements of greatness in him. The figures of Italian Senecan tragedy have not much more life than the ghosts with whom their plays usually open. Seneca's own Medea, not to seek any greater comparison, is a much more powerfully conceived character than any of them. Italian tragedy had to wait for the opera before it really found itself, a development which occurred only after the Renaissance period.

The French theatre, after a lively start with some amusing farces, produced nothing of lasting value at this time. Their plays are a pale reproduction of the classicism of the Italians, and they entirely lacked the Italian gift of comedy. External circumstances may have played some part in this lack of dramatic achievement in France. Theatrical production was closely restricted, and the popular stage, unlike that of England and Spain, sank into insignificance. In Italy, the drama was mostly aristocratic also, but there the rivalry of the ducal courts stimulated dramatic excellence.

Spanish and English comedy, as they developed out of the morality-play stage, had to learn form and structure. In part, they learned it the same way the Italians had, that is, from Latin comedy; but by the time they were ready to learn the lesson, Italian comedy was waiting for them side by side with the classics. Thus the latecomers in the field borrowed from both of them indiscriminately. But they found that this new comedy often contained the same types of characters that they were already familiar with in their native medieval drama. The vice of the morality play joined easily with the parasite of Plautus and Ariosto.

Not only did the Spanish and English writers of comedy translate or adapt from Italian comedy; they also raided the Italian *novelle* again and again for plots. It was from the *novelle* that they got their romantic plot materials, stories of complications in love rather than in tricking old fathers or uncles. In the romantic comedies, women became much more important, as can be seen strikingly in both Lope de Vega and Shakespeare. In this new type of comedy, unknown in the world before, witty conversation is mixed with lyrical love-making, and lower-class characters are commonly introduced for humor. Thus, it did for drama what Ariosto had done for narrative poetry. Satirical comedy was not at all unknown, but only in Ben Jonson did it rise to the level of a great moral force, tearing the mask from hypocrisy, greed, and meanness—and Jonson comes at the very end of the period.

We have already seen that Italian tragedy failed because of too close an adherence to Senecan form and classical stories. Again, England and Spain, though not France, showed themselves able to learn the lesson of form without allowing it to impede their free development towards something new. Following the normal human desire to see things acted out, they abolished messengers and offstage action and brought all the essential incidents before the eyes of the audience. Next, they soon began to interest themselves not in the fall of a lurid Senecan villain but in the fall of a good or partially good man, which is much more interesting. This the Greeks might have taught them, but there is no evidence that the Greeks did; they worked it out slowly and painfully for themselves. So, for Renaissance dramatists, the point of interest came to be the steps by which a relatively good man is led to crime or disaster. Motive becomes the essential thing, and yet so vigorous was the interest in fullblooded life at that time that the study of motive was never divorced, as it so often is today, from stirring action upon the stage. The treatment of motives was facilitated and made more interesting by the abandonment of the classical unity of time. Mr. W. H. Auden has recently pointed out that in most classical tragedies the hero is already caught in the trap, since the action occurs on the last day only, and we do not see him making the choices which lead to his downfall. But in Shakespeare, Marlowe, and Tirso da Molina, we watch the hero create his own tragic dilemma. Macbeth need not burden his conscience with murder and usurpation unless he wills to do so within the compass of the play; Faustus may always repent if he will assert his trust in God's mercy. Tirso's sinner in *El Condenado por desconfiado* (The Doubter Damned) does repent. These and many other protagonists in Spanish and English tragedy actively work out their own fates within the compass of the play. They not only suffer; they prepare their own suffering.

The preoccupation of the sixteenth century with religious issues provided a good climate for tragedy. Man's eternal fate as well as his temporal end was ever in the minds of both writers and audiences. The religious themes of Marlowe and Tirso da Molina show this. The whole power of Tirso's conception of the Don Juan story lies in the fact that there is a moral power in the universe against which Don Juan rebels in his every act and thought, in the fact that hell does await him, as it does Faustus. This is true, too, in Shakespeare, even though Shakespeare does not openly deal with religious themes.

In Shakespeare we may say that Renaissance tragedy reaches its height; but, rather significantly, this height is reached after 1600. The development of tragedy in the sixteenth century was very slow and by the time it came to its complete fruition a new and more sombre spirit was coming in. We see the same thing happening in Ben Jonson's great comedies and in Cervantes' *Don Quixote.* The difference can easily be observed by comparing the lyrical optimism of *Romeo and Juliet* with the questioning spirit of *Macbeth* and *Lear.* In Shakespeare's tragedies, man is seen at his noblest. He makes mistakes, he sins against heaven and his fellow man, he falls; but he falls not weakly or in disgrace; he falls as only one can fall who was created but a little lower than the angels. And he falls with his free will intact.

We have now observed the progress of Renaissance litera-ture as it spread through Europe. What generalizations can

one make about it considered as a whole? Sound generalizations are difficult enough when one is considering only a single
country. To draw general conclusions about four different
literatures, even though within the same historical period, is
highly dangerous.

The criterion of individualism is of dubious value, even
when applied to Renaissance life as a whole. Certainly, when
applied to the literature alone, it offers little help. Great
literature has always been concerned with great individuals.
And the example of Marlowe's supermen is misleading.
Renaissance literature as a whole is not characterized by figures in rebellion against religion or society.

In the nineteenth century the Renaissance was often interpreted on its literary side by stressing the revival of the
classics. This is an aspect which needs to be examined with
great care. The classics certainly were revived and reinter-
preted. Many writers were influenced by the Stoic philosophy
of Cicero and Seneca and many more were influenced by
classic ideas of form in the epic and the drama. But we should
be careful to remember that this in itself did not bring about
the new literature. The names of Dante, Petrarch, Boccaccio,
and Chaucer—all of them coming before the classical revival
of the fifteenth century—show that the new literature would
have appeared in any case. What the classical influence accomplished was to speed up the achievement of form and
style on the part of Renaissance writers. Even this kind of
influence was far from being a dominating force. Ariosto
accepted classical dramatic form in his comedies but rejected
it entirely in his *Orlando Furioso*. In fact, all the attempts
to write epics in the classical form at this period were failures.
Only Tasso, who came after the Italian Renaissance had run
its course, succeeded in this. The English parallel is Milton.
In the drama the influence of the classics was of great importance, but only as a contributing influence. The predecessors
and contemporaries of Lope de Vega and Shakespeare wrote
better plays because of their knowledge of Latin drama, but

they did not, like the Italians, pay any very strict regard to classical form. The really great classical drama, that of the Greeks, had almost no influence at all. Finally, it should be noted that attempts to use classical subject matter were almost always failures, whereas many great Renaissance literary works are composed of medieval subject matter. In spite of the humanists, the creative artist seemed to feel at home in the medieval world, but was a stranger, albeit an admiring one, in the ancient world.

Another feature often assigned to the Renaissance is the rise of secularism. This is, of course, true when applied to the whole life of the period as compared to the Middle Ages. Yet Renaissance literature, when compared to that of any period other than the Middle Ages, is not more, but less, secular. It is true that the Renaissance hero does not attend Mass before every exploit, and he has not had a vision of the Holy Grail, but he is in many ways more religious than Odysseus or Aeneas, and certainly more genuinely devoted to God than the agonized self-worshipping Romantic hero. In this connection the influence of Neoplatonism in supporting the spiritual tone of creative literature must not be overlooked.

I feel on safer ground in pointing to the tremendous outpouring of the creative spirit in the Renaissance, a spirit found in every aspect of its life: the rise of national patriotism, the thrust toward power of the upper middle class, the expansion of the geographical world through voyages of discovery. This same spirit is found in all the arts at this time: painting, sculpture, architecture, music, and literature. All were determined to produce new and more ambitious masterpieces. And this is particularly true of the two great national states, Spain and England. In neither of these countries were writers overwhelmed by the achievements of Italy. Ariosto may be magnificent, but Spenser hopes to outdo him—and, of course, ends by doing something quite different. Italian comedy may be highly amusing, but Lope de Vega will show them something new with the love-making of his witty society ladies. Senecan revenge tragedy may be a very smooth product in the hands of the clever Italians, but Shakespeare will show them a tragedy full of real life and genuine nobility.

And just at the time that this great burst of creative power exploded upon Europe there arose a new conception of romantic love which, like the medieval concept of courtly love, came into conflict with social organization, but in a very different way. Courtly love, built upon adultery, had threatened the family and the teachings of the Church. The new romantic love was built upon marriage, but it conflicted with parental authority, with the right of the parent to arrange a suitable, or perhaps a profitable, marriage for his children. This new conception of love was stimulating to writers in many ways. It provided a scheme within which love plots could be handled without condoning immorality, while, on the other hand, it offered countless varieties of conflict with other human beings and with fate which could be used in complicating the plot. It provided a definite climax in the successful marriage of the pair, whereas the older courtly love plot must either end in tragedy or find itself vainly seeking for a climax. Thus, while Spenser and Tasso both exploit the new theory of love in their epics, it is in romantic comedy that it finds its greatest expression. In spite of the brilliant exceptions of *Romeo and Juliet* and *Othello,* most Renaissance tragedies deal with larger themes than private love. The introduction of a love theme into the Faustus legend was reserved for the Romantic age.

It is trite but true to say that the Renaissance was an age of transition. Its literature is full of medieval materials and medieval conventions, but it is informed with a new spirit which was to lead it irresistibly, in the centuries to come, into a full-fledged literature of the modern world. It has become aware of realism of presentation, just as Renaissance art had become aware of perspective, but it has not yet sold out completely to realism. It is at home still in allegory, in theology, and in a kind of poetry which has not surrendered to the dialect of the man in the street. It may seem very hard-boiled in its Machiavellis, its Bacons, and its Benvenuto Cellinis, but it has not relinquished the spiritual aspirations of the Middle Ages. Its Martin Luthers and its Ignatius Loyolas show that, and so does the movingly beautiful prose of Cranmer's *Book of Common Prayer*. These men knew the thirst of the soul, which, as Ben Jonson said, doth ask a drink divine.

Author's note to ARTIST, SCIENTIST, GENIUS: NOTES ON THE "RENAISSANCE-DÄMMERUNG" by Erwin Panofsky

AUTHOR'S NOTE: *The present paper is a revised version of a lecture first delivered, under the same title, at the Metropolitan Museum of Art in 1952 and preliminarily published in* THE RENAISSANCE, A SYMPOSIUM, FEBRUARY 8-10, 1952, *New York, 1953, p. 77 ff. (cf. also the abstracts in* RENAISSANCE NEWS, *V, 1952, p. 5 ff., and* INTERNATIONAL CONGRESS ON THE HISTORY OF ART, AMSTERDAM, 1952, ACTES, *The Hague, 1955, p. 29 f.).*

Apart from the correction of obvious errors and some minor stylistic changes, Sections I and II have been considerably shortened because their content was incorporated, in much expanded and documented form, in a book entitled RENAISSANCE AND RENASCENCES IN WESTERN ART, *Stockholm, 1960, pp. 1-41. Conversely, a few additions have been made (see particularly pp. 160, 177, 178 Figs. 18, 25, 26. The original Section III has been deleted.*

I have, however, not seen any reason to modify my position in principle, and this applies particularly to the objections raised by Professor Harcourt Brown, "The Renaissance and Historians of Science," STUDIES IN THE RENAISSANCE, *VII, 1960, p. 27 ff. Professor Brown largely limits himself to a defense of what the late George Sarton had said some thirty years ago (J. W. Thompson, et al.,* THE CIVILIZATION OF THE RENAISSANCE, *Chicago, 1929, p. 75 ff.) and goes so far as to state, on p. 42: "Sarton never withdrew his fundamental view that the so-called Renaissance was an episode between two creative ages [viz., the fourteenth and the seventeenth centuries]." He fails, however, to inform his readers that Sarton was not only "in the audience" when the Symposium of 1952 was held but contributed a paper entitled "The Quest for Truth: A Brief Account of Scientific Progress during the Renaissance" (cf. pp. 55 ff.; abstract in* RENAISSANCE NEWS, *V, 1952, p. 7). And here the same Sarton who in 1929 had claimed that, as far as science was concerned, the Renaissance was "an anticlimax between two peaks" says, by way of introduction to the discussion of twelve different fields of scientific endeavor: "In the field of science the novelties were gigantic, revolutionary . . . the Renaissance scientists introduced not a 'new look' but a new being. The novelty was often so great that one could hardly speak of a Renaissance or rebirth; it was a real birth, a new beginning."*

VI ARTIST, SCIENTIST, GENIUS: NOTES ON THE "RENAISSANCE-DÄMMERUNG"

by Erwin Panofsky

I

For many centuries we have been in the habit of dividing the history of the Western world into three major "periods": Antiquity, the Middle Ages and a "Modern Era" beginning with a phase known as the Renaissance. The first age to define and name itself, this Renaissance claimed to have reverted to nature and the classical past after a long estrangement from both.

Of late, there has developed a tendency either to minimize this claim or to disallow it altogether—so much so that the very fact that there ever was such a thing as the Renaissance has been contested. No one, of course, would question that the Renaissance was linked to the Middle Ages (which, incidentally, owes its very name to the Renaissance) by a thousand ties. But the art historian, at least, finds it impossible to abandon the proposition that something really decisive—to use the biological term, a "mutational change'"—did happen in the three centuries between *ca.* 1300 and *ca.* 1600.

When we look at the Pantheon of *ca.* 125 A.D., Our Lady's Church at Treves (one of the rare central-plan structures produced by the Gothic period) of *ca.* 1250 A.D., and Palladio's "Villa Rotonda" of *ca.* 1550 A.D., we cannot help realizing that, all differences notwithstanding, the "Villa Rotonda" has more in common with the Pantheon than with Our Lady's Church at Treves even though more than fourteen hundred years had passed between the "Villa Rotonda" and the Pantheon, and only about three hundred between the "Villa Rotonda" and Our Lady's at Treves.

Likewise, when we consider the image of a lion drawn by a French artist named Villard de Honnecourt of about 1235 (and, as he proudly asserts in writing, "portrayed from life")[1] we cannot but feel a difference in kind rather than degree between his work and the silver-point sketch of a lion produced (also "from life") by Albrecht Dürer[2] in 1521 (Figs. 1 and 2).

II

This new approach to the visible world—including the visible remnants of classical sculpture and architecture—was predicated upon a new definition of artistic construction and representation as such, a definition which began to be applied in practice from about 1300 and was rationalized into a philosophical and mathematical theory some one hundred or one hundred and twenty years later. The Middle Ages had conceived of a picture—be it a mural, book illumination, panel painting or even a stained glass window—as a material, impenetrable surface *on* which figures and things are depicted. With the fathers of Italian Trecento painting, notably Giotto and Duccio, the picture began to be thought of, as Leone Battista Alberti was to formulate it about 1435, as an imaginary windowpane *through* which we look out into a section of space (Fig. 3).[3] And since perspective is a matter of art as well as geometry this leads us right *in medias res.*

[1] H. R. Hahnloser, *Villard de Honnecourt, Kritische Gesamtausgabe des Bauhüttenbuches, MS. fr.* 19093 *der Pariser Nationalbibliothek,* Vienna, 1935, Pl. 48.

[2] F. Lippmann, *Zeichnungen von Albrecht Dürer in Nachbildungen,* Berlin, 1883-1929, No. 425.

[3] *Leone Battista Alberti, Della Pittura,* L. Mallé, ed., Florence, 1950, pp. 65, 70; quoted in E. Panofsky, *Renaissance and Renascences,* p. 120, Note 1. See also Leonardo da Vinci (J. P. Richter, *The Literary Works of Leonardo da Vinci,* London, 1883; second edition by Irma Richter, London, 1939), No. 83, where the picture plane is likened to a "pariete di vetro." The practical application of this simile—viz., an apparatus by means of which the painter can sketch

LEO

þest · 1 · lion si con̄
on le voit p̄ dettant
⁊ sacies bien q̄l fu
conttefais al uif·

þesc · 1 · potc espī·
cest une bestelete·
q̄ lance se soit q̄ant
ele ⁊ conette·

1. Villard de Honnecourt, *Lion* (Paris, Bibliothèque Nationale, MS.
fr. 19093, fol. 24v, *ca.* 1230-35).

From what has been said, it is evident that the art historian cannot possibly accept that radical thesis according to which the Renaissance did not exist at all. He can, and must, however, attempt to come to terms with the more moderate view to the effect that there was a distinct and definable period, holding an intermediary position between the Middle Ages and the Modern era and extending, to mention a few sig-

2. Albrecht Dürer, *Lion* (drawing L.425, Vienna, Albertina).

nificant names, from Giotto and Duccio to Caravaggio and the Carracci brothers in painting, and from Ockham and Buridan to Galileo and Kepler in the sciences; but that this period, while representing a magnificent climax in the arts,

---

upon an actual glass plate the object before him—also seems to have been suggested by Leonardo (Richter, No. 523). Apparatuses of this kind were subsequently perfected by Dürer (woodcut B.146, our Fig. 3) and others, and they were employed by portraitists from Bramantino and Holbein to Emil Orlik.

represented an "anticlimax between two peaks" in the sciences.[4]

Is it not possible that the whole idea of a clean-cut separation between artistic and scientific activities must be re-examined when we deal with the Renaissance? Is it not possible that at this stage of European history a science whose specu-

3. Albrecht Dürer, *Painter Making a Portrait from Life with the Aid of a Glass Plate* (Woodcut B.146, 1525).

lative efforts had thus far, by and large, not sought support in empirical research and which was just beginning to turn "experimental," and an art whose practical procedures had thus far, by and large, not sought support in a systematic theory and which was just beginning to claim a position

[4] For this phrase, coined by George Sarton in 1929, see p. 122, Author's Note.

among the "Artes Liberales" by doing precisely this—that such a science and such an art advanced, as it were, on a united front? Should we not give the allegedly less productive sciences some credit for the results achieved by the admittedly flourishing arts and, more important, consider some of the achievements of the arts to be vital contributions to the progress of the sciences? In short, should we not realize that the Renaissance was a period of *decompartmentalization*: a period which broke down the barriers that had kept things in order —but also apart—during the Middle Ages? And that it thus produced an untold variety of mixtures and interpenetrations which, seen in retrospect, may either look like synthesis or like chaos, depending on whether the newly created compounds proved to be stable or unstable, when another process of compartmentalization set in with the seventeenth century?

III

One small but significant example of compartmentalization and decompartmentalization is that curious "law of disjunction," by virtue of which medieval art and, to a somewhat lesser extent, medieval literature, consistently separated classical form from classical subject matter: Madonnas or patriarchs could borrow their appearance from classical statues or reliefs while the classical gods or heroes appeared in the guise of medieval knights and scholars, and it was left to the Renaissance to reintegrate what the Middle Ages had set asunder.[5]

In this particular case the Renaissance produced what I have called a "stable compound"—meaning that the integration of classical form and classical subject matter, once achieved, was not to break apart again. This we can readily understand. What Raphael and Titian accomplished was not so much an innovatory synthesis as the restoration of a pre-existent unity, and this accomplishment was part and parcel

[5] For a fuller discussion of this "law of disjunction," see Panofsky, *Renaissance and Renascences*, pp. 84-113.

of a much broader development. The Middle Ages, not knowing that it was the Middle Ages, could not as yet visualize the pre-Christian past at a distance, and this is precisely what the Renaissance was able to do. Looking back at the pagan world from a quasi-historical point of view much as the Renaissance artists looked at the visible world from a perspective point of view, and projecting this image onto an ideal projection plane, the Renaissance humanists learned to think of classical civilization as a totality. And it is no accident that they expressed this totality by such collective nouns as *antiquitas* or even *sacrosancta vetustas*—nouns which, so far as I know, have no analogy in medieval Latin and carry entirely different implications in classical Latin.

But the "decompartmentalizing" tendency of the Renaissance was by no means satisfied with reintegrating what had originally been united and had come to be broken up *ex post facto*. The Renaissance "decompartmentalized" of its own accord, so to speak, and of the much more ambitious compounds thus produced some proved to be unstable.

The most important among these unstable compounds is what is known as the Neoplatonic (as a matter of fact, Neo-Neoplatonic) movement originated by Marsilio Ficino in Florence about 1460 and catching on like wildfire—a movement the impact of which can be compared, in range and intensity, only with that of psychoanalysis today. Medieval thought had endeavored to *incorporate* whatever seemed admissible of classical ideas and yet to draw as sharp a line as possible between reason and faith. The Neoplatonists, however, attempted to *fuse* two cultural worlds clearly recognized as distinct from each other (the very title of Ficino's major work, *Theologia Platonica*, would not have been possible even in the twelfth century), yet to abolish the borderline not only between philosophy, religion and magic but between all kinds of philosophies, all kinds of religions and all kinds of magic, including Hermeticism, Orphism, Pythagore-

ism, Cabala, and the ancient mysteries of Egypt and India.[6]
This wild mixture could not resist the criticism, both scientific and philological, which was to set in during the seventeenth century. But we should not forget that in this case, too,
chaos was the prerequisite of order. It was only the indiscrimi-
nate acceptance of too many kinds of Platonism which made
it necessary to isolate the real Plato from all the later accre-
tions (the first to perceive this problem was, characteristically,
the great Leibniz). And the inherent animism and pan-
psychism of a doctrine which looked upon the universe as an
"animal more living and more unified than any other animal"
served the advance of modern science in indirect fashion: it
undermined, for example, the long unchallenged theory of
the four humors and thereby opened new vistas in biology
and medicine; it paved the way to Servetus' discovery of the
pulmonary transit;[7] and, most important, it broke the spell
of the essential dichotomy that had been believed to exist between an imperfect, corruptible earth and the perfect, incor-
ruptible heavens. The Neoplatonists thus unwittingly prepared the minds for Galileo's triumphant announcement that
the stars are made of the same stuff and obey the same laws
as our "vile earth."[8]

The Neoplatonic attempt to reconcile the irreconcilable,
then, could not endure—except in poetry and aesthetics where
the influence of Neoplatonic thought made itself felt from
the metaphysical poets to Goethe and Mallarmé, from
Boileau to the English and German Romanticists.

Another synthesis, however, producing as it were the very
antidote to the Neoplatonic poison, proved to be stable: the

[6] For an excellent summary of these syncretistic tendencies, see F. A.
Yates, *The French Academies of the Sixteenth Century* (Studies of the
Warburg Institute, XV), London 1947, p. 2 ff.

[7] R. Bainton, "Michael Servetus and the Pulmonary Transit of the
Blood," *Bulletin of the History of Medicine*, XXV, 1951, p. 1 ff.

[8] See H. Baron, "Towards a More Positive Evaluation of the Fifteenth-Century Renaissance," *Journal of the History of Ideas*, IV,
1943, p. 21 ff., particularly p. 33 ff.

elimination of the barriers which in the Middle Ages had separated the "liberal arts" from the "mechanical" ones—theoretical insight, which was supposed to be a matter of the pure intellect, and practical pursuits, including the representational arts, which were supposed to be a matter of mere sensory perception and manual skill.

IV

From the beginning, the Renaissance writers on art untiringly repeat, like a *symbolum fidei*, the statement that practice must be based on theory and that, as Dürer puts it, "The one without the other is of no avail."[9] This statement sounds like a truism; but by medieval standards it was a revolutionary postulate. For in the Middle Ages there was no functional interaction between artistic practice and artistic theory.

What the Middle Ages had called *perspectiva*, was only optics, that is to say, an elaborate theory of vision which attempted to determine the structure of the natural visual image by mathematical means but did not attempt to teach

[9] Dürer in the so-called "Aesthetic Excursus" in his *Treatise on Human Proportions* (K. Lange and F. Fuhse, *Albrecht Dürers schriftlicher Nachlass*, Halle, 1893, p. 230, line 1 ff.): "Understanding (*verstand*) must grow together with practice (*gebrauch*) so that the hand can do what the will in the understanding wants to be done. From this there results, in time, a certainty (*gewissheit*) both in theory (*kunst*) and practice. These two must be together, for the one without the other is of no avail." For statements such as these, which could be multiplied *ad infinitum*, and Dürer's and his contemporaries' use of the word *kunst*, see E. Panofsky, *Dürers Kunsttheorie, vornehmlich in ihrem Verhältnis zur Kunsttheorie der Italiener*, Berlin, 1915, p. 169 ff. (cf. also E. Panofsky, *Albrecht Dürer*, first edition Princeton, 1943, I, pp. 242 ff., 273). We should remember that even Leonardo, the self-styled empiricist, insists on the complementary relation between theory and practice and stresses the supremacy of the former: theory is compared to the captain, practice to the soldiers; and a practitioner lacking in theoretical knowledge is likened to a pilot without rudder or compass.

the artist how to reproduce this image in a painting or drawing. Even the great Trecento masters obtained their results in an entirely unscientific manner: they made the vanishing lines converge in one point only when such a con-

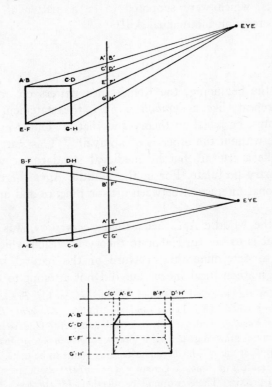

4. Perspective Construction of a Parallelepiped according to Brunelleschi.

vergence was particularly obvious (viz., within the unobstructed section of one plane) and determined the sequence of the transversal lines by rule of thumb, often mechanically diminishing the distance between one transversal and the next by one-third. It was not until about 1420 that Filippo Brunelleschi placed perspective on a truly scientific basis: he

conceived of the painting as a plane cross section through the
pencil of rays connecting the eye of the painter (and the beholder) with the object or objects seen. This cross section
could be constructed by exact geometrical methods, and it

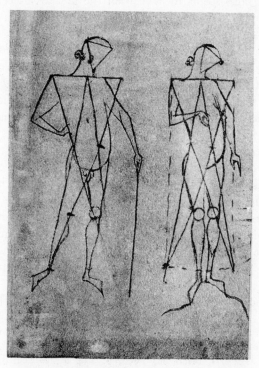

5. Villard de Honnecourt, *Construction of Human
Figures* (Paris, Bibliothèque Nationale, MS.
fr. 19093, fol. 18, *ca.* 1230-35).

was this construction which laid the foundation for what was
to develop into both projective and analytical geometry.[10] It

[10] For the development of perspective (now contested in several respects though unanimity has been reached about the points stressed in
the text), see E. Panofsky, *Renaissance and Renascences*, pp. 120-140,
with bibliography on p. 122 f.

is, in fact, in the perspective constructions of the Italian Renaissance that we can discover the roots of what we call a system of coordinates, and it is more than a coincidence that the same Brunelleschi who invented scientific perspective (Fig. 4) also seems to have been the first architect to draw ground plans and elevations to scale by means of a uniform grill of squares.[11]

What scientific perspective (now called *perspectiva artificialis* as opposed to the old science of optics, which was now designated as *perspectiva naturalis* or *perspectiva communis*) did for space in general, an equally new discipline did for the individual object, particularly the human and animal body: the theory of proportions.

A medieval author such as Villard de Honnecourt tells his fellow craftsmen how to determine the proportions of a figure as well as its contours by means of a handy schematization (Fig. 5); Alberti, Leonardo and Dürer take the measurements of living human beings and tabulate the results in terms of numbers and graphs (Fig. 6), thereby transforming a device of draftsmanship into a mathematical and statistical science which was to develop into anthropometry[12] and physiognomics.

In short, the Renaissance bridged the gap which had sepa-

---

[11] For Brunelleschi as a perspectivist and as the inaugurator of scaled architectural drawings, see R. Krautheimer and T. Krautheimer-Hess, *Lorenzo Ghiberti*, Princeton, 1956, p. 234 ff., particularly p. 238; cf. F. D. Prager, "Brunelleschi's Inventions and the Renewal of Roman Masonry Work," *Osiris*, IX, 1950, p. 457 ff.

[12] For the history of the theory of proportions see E. Panofsky, "The History of the Theory of Proportions as a Reflection of the History of Styles," *Meaning in the Visual Arts*, Anchor paperback, 1955, pp. vi, 55 ff. (cf. also E. Panofsky, *Albrecht Dürer*, I, pp. 261 ff., 296). It should be noted that Dürer is unique in supplementing the rich statistical material presented in the first two Books of his *Treatise on Human Proportions* by an elaborate theory of variation which was revived in no less serious and famous a work than D'Arcy W. Thompson's *On Growth and Form*, first published in 1917.

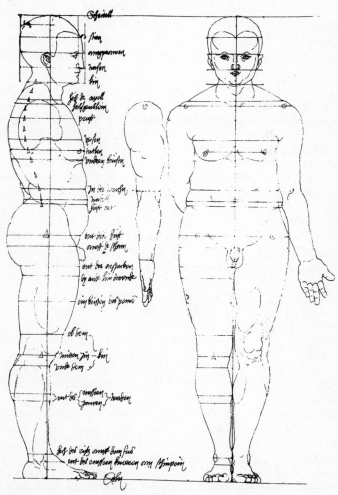

6. Albrecht Dürer, *Study in Human Proportion*, (Drawing: auto-tracing, Cambridge, Mass., Fogg Art Museum, about 1523).

rated the scholar and thinker from the practitioner; it has
been said, not without justification, that in the Renaissance
the greatest advances in natural science were made by engineers, instrument-makers and artists rather than professors.[13]
It was the absence of interaction between manual and intellectual methods which had prevented the admirable inven-

[13] What may be called the operational explanation of the genesis of
"modern" science (for the opposite point of view, see E. A. Burtt,
*The Metaphysics of Sir Isaac Newton: An Essay in the Metaphysical
Foundations of Modern Science*, London and New York, 1925) was
already outlined by L. Olschki, *Geschichte der neusprachlichen wissen-
schaftlichen Literatur*, Heidelberg, 1918-1927, III, *passim*. It
was systematically advocated by E. W. Strong, *Procedures and Mathematics: A Study in the Philosophy of Mathematical and Physical Science
in the Sixteenth and Seventeenth Centuries*, Berkeley, 1936, and
(independently of Strong) by E. Zilsel, "The Origins of Gilbert's
Method," *Journal of the History of Ideas*, II, 1941, p. 1 ff. (cf. *Zilsel*,
"The Genesis of the Concept of Scientific Progress," *Journal of the History of Ideas*, VI, 1945, p. 324 ff.). While the facts marshalled by
Olschki, Strong, Zilsel and others cannot be disputed we should not
forget that purely operational procedures (primarily destined to cope
with the concrete task of mastering nature) and purely theoretical
speculation are not mutually exclusive but complementary; see E.
Cassirer, "Mathematische Mystik und mathematische Naturwissenschaft;
Betrachtungen zur Entstehungsgeschichte der exakten Wissenschaft,"
Lychnos, 1940, p. 248 ff. It should also be noted that the basic process
correctly stressed by Zilsel, viz., the demolition of social barriers be-
tween manual and intellectual labor, was first achieved by the artists
(who tend to be neglected by Zilsel as well as Strong). Even in the
Middle Ages not only the musician but also the architect had been
ranked extremely high (see N. Pevsner, "The Term 'Architect' in the
Middle Ages," *Speculum*, XVII, 1942, p. 549 ff.; E. Panofsky, *Gothic
Architecture and Scholasticism*, Latrobe, 1951, p. 25 f., Fig. 1; P.
Frankl, *The Gothic: Literary Sources and Interpretations through Eight
Centuries*, Princeton, 1960, p. 135 ff.); and in the Renaissance the
privileges previously accorded only to those who mastered one of the
artes liberales were claimed by and extended to painters and sculptors
from the beginning of the fifteenth century, long before a comparable
position was achieved by "surgeons, navigators, and makers of nautical
and musical instruments."

tions of medieval engineers and craftsmen from being noticed by what were then called the "natural philosophers" and which, conversely, had prevented the equally admirable deductions of logicians and mathematicians from being tested by experiment. Well-founded doubts had been raised, particularly from the twelfth century, against Aristotle's theory of motion, especially his contention that the speed of falling bodies varies in proportion to their weight; but no one prior to the sixteenth century seems to have thought of throwing two objects of different weight from a tower and seeing what would happen.[14]

[14] There has been some discussion, first, as to whether Aristotle really asserted that the speed of falling bodies varied in proportion to their weight; second, as to whether Galileo really attempted to demonstrate the opposite by experiment; third, as to whether he was the first to do so. See, e.g., L. Cooper, *Aristotle, Galileo and the Tower of Pisa*, Ithaca, 1935, devastatingly reviewed by H. F. Cherniss, *Modern Language Notes*, LI, 1936, p. 184 f.; H. A. Wolfson, *Crescas' Critique of Aristotle*, Cambridge, 1929; Olschki, *op. cit.*, II, pp. 130, 254 ff.; E. Moody, "Galileo and Avempace," *Journal of the History of Ideas*, XII, 1951, pp. 163 ff., 375 ff. As a result of this discussion, we can take it as established, first, that Aristotle did hold the erroneous view traditionally ascribed to him; second, that doubts against this view were raised from a very early date (Philoponus) and vigorously stated by such medieval thinkers as Thomas Aquinas, Duns Scotus, Avempace and, perhaps most sophisticatedly, Hasdai Crescas (1340-1410); third, that these doubts were never tested by experiment throughout the Middle Ages; fourth, that Galileo did make experiments to disprove the Aristotelian theory but was by no means the first to do so: in his *Questione sull' alchimia* (unpublished during his lifetime) Benedetto Varchi (well known to art historians from his *Due Lezzioni*, Florence, 1549, the first dealing with Michelangelo, the second containing the replies to a questionnaire referring to the relative merits of sculpture and painting) writes as follows (here quoted after Olschki, *loc. cit.*): "While most modern philosophers believe but never demonstrate what is written by good authors, particularly Aristotle, it may be no less safe and instructive to reverse the process and occasionally to resort to experience, for instance, as regards the motion of bodies. In this respect Aristotle and all the other philosophers believed, without

It should be borne in mind, however, that this absence of interaction between manual and intellectual methods was only one aspect of compartmentalization in general. Even within one scientific field there was a curious lack of transmission belts, as when astronomical observations and calculations, often surprisingly accurate, were hardly ever linked up with theoretical speculations, often surprisingly penetrating, on celestial mechanics. The Renaissance introduced such transmission belts, not only between but also within the manual and intellectual spheres. We can observe the formation of groups and friendships conducive to cross-fertilization between all kinds of people, including the much-maligned humanists; on the other hand, we can observe a combination of many interests in one and the same person. Antonio di Tuccio di Marabottino Manetti was a humanist; but as a friend of Brunelleschi and Paolo Toscanelli he raised and discussed the eminently "perspective" question as to the exact location, shape and measurements of Dante's Hell—a question later to be taken up by the Dante commentator, Alessandro Vellutello, and finally submitted to the judgment of no less a man than

---

any doubt, that a body falls the more speedily the heavier it is, which is not borne out by experiment. And if I were not afraid to stray too far from my subject I should spend more time to confirming this view [viz., the anti-Aristotelian position] which is shared by others, for example, the Rev. Father Francesco Beato, Professor of Metaphysics at Pisa and a learned philosopher as well as a good theologian, and Messer Luca Ghini, the excellent physician and botanist, whom I have heard lecturing in public at the University of Bologna." Thus it remains true what Wolfson (*op. cit.*, p. 127) wrote in 1929: "Crescas had passed the stage when man condemned reason; he had reached the stage when man began to doubt reason, but he had not yet entered the stage when man learned to control reason by facts." And that Galileo was not the first to "climb up to the top of a tower" and to "watch the landing of two unequal weights" tends to show only that this third stage was reached, or at least was about to be reached, several decades before he was born.

Galileo.[15] Fracastoro, one of the real geniuses in medicine, was also an astronomer, a literary critic and an excellent poet, and his self-chosen emblem was an altar dedicated to Aesculapius, Minerva and Apollo.[16] Pirckheimer, the philologist and antiquarian, knew enough mathematics to initiate his bosom friend, Albrecht Dürer, into Eutocius' Commentary upon Archimedes—while Dürer, the painter, wrote a geometrical treatise which was respectfully quoted by Galileo and Kepler.[17] Even Leonardo was not so illiterate as he would have us believe:[18] the very Galenisms for which he has been taken to task by modern critics prove that he had read Galen who, like Archimedes, was then a "modern" author, rediscovered by the humanists.[19]

[15] See the Introduction to *Le Opere di Galileo Galilei*, IX (Edizione Nazionale, A. Favaro, ed., Florence, 1899), pp. 7-10. Galileo's own *Due Lezioni . . . circa la figura, sito e grandezza dell' Inferno di Dante* are reprinted pp. 28-57.

[16] For Fracastoro, see F. Saxl, "Pagan Sacrifice in the Italian Renaissance," *Journal of the Warburg Institute*, II, 1939, p. 346 ff. (p. 357 f.) and *Enciclopedia Italiana*, XV (1949 edition), p. 829 f.

[17] See E. Panofsky, *Albrecht Dürer*, pp. 253-260.

[18] For the reservations that must be placed on Leonardo's own, only half-serious self-characterization as an "omo sanza lettere," see A. Chastel, "Léonard et la culture," *Léonard de Vinci et l'expérience scientifique au XVIᵉ siècle, Colloques Internationaux du Centre de la Recherche Scientifique, Sciences Humaines*, Paris, 1953 (hereafter to be referred to as *"Léonard, Colloques"*), p. 251 ff. Conversely, it is impossible to make Leonardo a Neoplatonist as does F. M. Bongioanni, *Leonardo Pensatore; Saggio sulla posizione filosofica di Leonardo da Vinci*, Piacenza, 1935. For an excellent analysis of Leonardo's essentially anti- or para-Platonic attitude (which this writer has stressed from his doctoral dissertation and will not cease to stress), see G. de Santillana, "Léonard et ceux qu'il n'a pas lus," *Léonard, Colloques*, p. 43 ff.

[19] It should be noted, in addition, that the greatest error caused by Leonardo's "préjugé galénique," viz., that he not only believed to have seen but actually drew the minute perforations of the heart's septum required by Galen's theory of pulsation (see, e.g., G. Sarton, "Léonard de Vinci, ingénieur et savant," *Léonard, Colloques*, p. 11 ff.,

In short, the tangibilization of science, if I may say so, was complementary to an intellectualization of all mechanical professions, pre-eminently the arts.[20] Much of that which was later to be isolated as "natural science" came into being in artists' studios. And, perhaps the most important point, the rise of those particular branches of natural science which may be called observational or descriptive—zoology, botany, palae-ontology, several aspects of physics and, first and foremost, anatomy—was so directly predicated upon the rise of the representational techniques that we should think twice before admitting that the Renaissance achieved great things in art while contributing little to the progress of science.

V

As late as 1502, a member of the medical faculty at Leipzig University courageously proposed that an "anatomy," that is

---

particularly p. 17), was shared by none other than Vesalius whose *Fabrica* of 1543 is hailed by Sarton himself (p. 15) as being "vraiment la base de l'anatomie moderne." For Leonardo's familiarity with and enthusiasm for Archimedes, see M. Johnson, "Pourquoi Léonard de Vinci cherchait-il les manuscrits scientifiques d'Archimède et comment les trouva-t-il?," *Léonard, Colloques*, p. 23 ff.

[20] The novel tendency toward "decompartmentalization" which, in my opinion, is characteristic of the Renaissance did not conflict but, on the contrary, helped to produce the equally novel tendency towards "specialization" which has been stressed by W. S. Heckscher, *Rembrandt's Anatomy of Dr. Nicolaas Tulp*, New York, 1958, pp. 60, 143 ff. (with rich bibliography on the general history of anatomical illustration). "Compartmentalization" amounts to the erection of mental barriers between methodically disparate fields of human endeavor; "specialization" to the refinement of technical skills (and consequently the division of labor) within a methodically unified field of human endeavor. It is precisely the rapprochement between speculative "natural philosophy" and practical experimentation which promoted, even necessitated, the rise of such specialties as those of the compass-makers (*circinarii*), watchmakers (*confectores horologii*), lens-grinders (*conspicillarii*), etc. In crucial cases, such as Galileo's, the scientist himself had to turn technician.

to say a dissection open to graduate students, be held at least every three years because "anyone who has not seen the inner arrangement of man is a physician only at great danger"; and about eight years later another member of the same faculty repeated this suggestion, still unheeded, with the remark that such dissections were the custom in Italy (*noch wellischer weysse.*)[21]

However, even in Italy—the "nurse of the intellect," as Vesalius calls her[22]—the practice of anatomy was of fairly recent origin. At Padua, the center of medical studies, the first public dissection (as opposed to occasional private autopsies which were performed whenever a person of consequence had died under mysterious circumstances) took place in 1341.[23] And even then dissections served the purpose of demonstration rather than investigation and were normally not performed by the professors themselves (Figs. 7 and 8). The knife was handled by a technical assistant; a "demonstrator"

[21] The suggestion of 1502 was made by Benedict Staatz, called Pistoris; that of about 1510 probably by Simon Pistoris. For both, see K. Sudhoff, *Die medizinische Fakultät zu Leipzig im ersten Jahrhundert der Universität*, Leipzig, 1909, pp. 44, 48.

[22] See L. Edelstein, "Andreas Vesalius, the Humanist," *Bulletin of the History of Medicine*, XIV, 1943, p. 547 ff. Vesalius wholeheartedly endorsed the humanistic "Geschichtskonstruktion" according to which his age was privileged to revive civilization after a long period of submersion, and he even looked upon his own work less as a new departure than as a restoration of the classical past: "Anatomy should be able to be recalled from the dead, so that, if it does not achieve with us a greater perfection than in any other place or time among the ancient teachers of anatomy, it might at least reach such a point that we could with confidence assert that our modern science of anatomy is equal to that of the old." See also E. Cassirer, "The Place of Vesalius in the Culture of the Renaissance," *Journal of Biology and Medicine*, XVI, 1943-44, p. 121 ff.

[23] See Sudhoff, *Die medizinische Fakultät*, p. 124. Cf. also Heckscher, *op. cit.*, particularly p. 42 ff.; A. M. Cetto, "Die Sektion in der mittelalterlichen Miniatur," *CIBA Symposium*, V, 1957, pp. 124 ff., 168 ff.

would direct the attention of the students to a particular detail by means of a pointer; and the professor, high up on his lectern, would read or recite a text regardless of whether it agreed with what could be observed with the eyes.

Small wonder, then, that painters rushed in where doctors feared to tread. Just about the time of that first Paduan "anatomy" the medical students examined the nudes produced by a pupil of Giotto, named Stefano, because they could learn therefrom what they could not in class.[24] And from the fifteenth century we have a continuous series of "painter-anatomists," running from Pollaiuolo to Michelangelo, Rosso Fiorentino and Alessandro Allori.

Leonardo da Vinci, who dissected more than thirty corpses, belongs to this series, and yet he does not. The other painter-anatomists, naturally concentrating their interest upon the bones, muscles and tendons which the professional physicians had understandably tended to neglect in favor of the intestines,[25] placed anatomy in the service of art; Leonardo placed art in the service of anatomy and thereby became the founder of anatomy as a science, based on extensive research, which aims to qualify not only the form but also the function of all human organs and to determine their variations accord-

[24] Filippo Villani (writing toward 1400), *De origine civitatis Florentiae et eiusdem famosis civibus* (J. von Schlosser, *Quellenbuch zur Kunstgeschichte des abendländischen Mittelalters*, Vienna, 1896, p. 371): "Stefanus, nature symia, tanta eius imitatione valuit, ut etiam a phisicis in figuratis per eum corporibus humanis arterie, vene, nervi queque minutissima liniamenta proprie colligantur."

[25] K. Sudhoff, "Tradition und Naturbeobachtung in den illustrierten medizinischen Handschriften und Frühdrucken, vornehmlich des XV. Jahrunderts," *Studien zur Geschichte der Medizin*, I, Leipzig, 1907, p. 59: "Muskelzeichnungen sind mir überhaupt nicht wiederbegegnet [*scil.*, after the entirely conventional, theologically-oriented "Treatise from Prüfening," dated 1158, and its thirteenth-century copy, clm. 13002 and 17403 (Sudhoff, Pls. XIII, XIV)] vor der Renaissance."

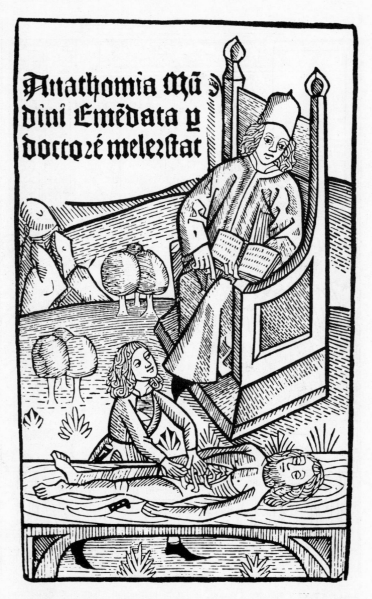

7. *Lesson in Anatomy* (Title Woodcut from Dr. Pollich of Mellerstadt, *Anathomia Mundini Emendata*, Leipzig, about 1493).

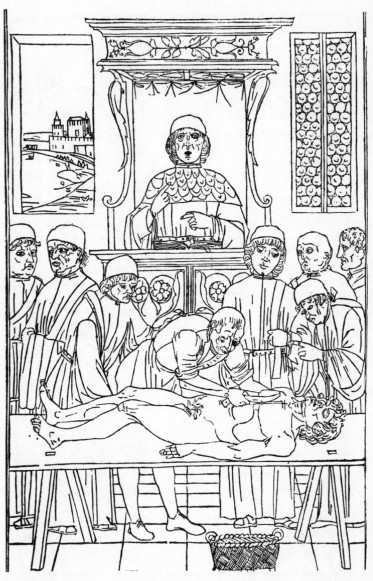

8. *Lesson in Anatomy* (Woodcut from Joannes de Ketham, *Fasciculus Medicinae*, Venice, 1493, fol. IIv.).

ing to age (from the fetal stage to extreme senescence), sex
and pathological conditions.[26]

That Leonardo was fully conscious of these aims we know
by his own words and deeds. But he was also conscious of the
fact—and in this respect he seems to have been the first—
that these aims could be reached only by new methods of
graphic representation. "And you who think to reveal," he
writes, "the figure of man in words, with his limbs arranged
in all their different attitudes, banish the idea from you, for
the more minute your description the more you will confuse
the mind of the reader and the more you will lead him away

[26] The literature on Leonardo as an anatomist, beginning with Vasari
in 1550 and Girolamo Cardano in 1553 (cf. Heckscher, *op. cit.*, p.
60), is practically boundless. Suffice it to list some of the more recent
publications: the pertinent contributions in *Leonardo da Vinci, Edizione
curata della Mostra di Leonardo da Vinci in Milano, Istituto Geografico
De Agostini*, Novara, *ca.* 1936 (particularly P. Emanuelli, "L'Anatomia
Vinciana," p. 205 ff.; G. Favaro, "L'Anatomia e le scienze biologiche,"
p. 363 ff.; C. F. Biaggi, "L'Anatomia artistica," p. 437 ff.); the pertinent chapters in A. Marazzo, ed., *Leonardo, Saggi e Ricerche, Istituto
Poligrafico dello Stato*, Rome, 1952, particularly E. D. Vitali,
"l'Anatomia e la fisiologia," p. 113 ff.; the pertinent chapter and
bibliographical references (pp. 121 ff., 185, 194) in L. H. Heydenreich, *Leonardo da Vinci*, London and Basel, 1954; Ch. H. D.
O'Malley and J. B. de C. M. Saunders, *Leonardo da Vinci on the
Human Body*, New York, 1952; S. Esche, *Leonardo da Vinci, Das
anatomische Werk (Ars Docta, VIII)*, Basel, 1954—for both these
works, see the important review by R. Herrlinger, entitled "Katalog
und Fragment, zwei neue Bücher über Leonardos Anatomie," in
Anatomischer Anzeiger, CIII, 1956, p. 153 ff.; E. Belt, *Leonardo the
Anatomist*, Lawrence, Kansas, 1955; "Les Dissections anatomiques de
Léonard de Vinci," *Léonard, Colloques*, p. 199 ff. For Leonardo's
gerontological efforts, see *idem*, "Leonardo da Vinci's Studies of the
Aging Process," *Raccolta Vinciana*, XVII, 1954, p. 91 ff. That Leonardo must also be considered the founder of comparative anatomy is
evident from a drawing such as Windsor 12625 (reproduced, e.g., in
Heydenreich, Fig. 192) and Windsor 12375 (reproduced *ibidem*,
Fig. 135) and several explicit verbal statements such as those quoted
by Belt, "Les Dissections anatomiques . . . ," p. 212 ff.

from the knowledge of the thing described. It is necessary therefore for you to represent and describe."[27] Among the qualifications of a good anatomist he lists, therefore, not only a strong stomach, perseverance and fearlessness in the presence of horrid corpses, but also the ability to calculate the dynamics of muscular movement, competent draftsmanship—and a command of perspective.[28]

[27] T. Sabachnikoff and G. Piumati, *I Manoscritti di Leonardo da Vinci della Reale Biblioteca di Windsor, Dell'Anatomia*, Fogli A, Paris, 1898, fol. 14v., here quoted after Heydenreich, *op. cit.*, p. 123.

[28] O. C. L. Vangensten *et al.*, *Leonardo da Vinci, Quaderni d'Anatomia*, Christiania, 1911-1914, I, fol. 13v. (often reprinted and translated, e.g., in Richter, *op. cit.*, No. 796); here quoted after Heydenreich, *op. cit.*, p. 125:

"And you who say that it is better to look at an anatomical demonstration than to see these drawings, you would be right, if it were possible to observe all the details shown in these drawings in a single figure, in which, with all your ability, you will not see nor acquire a knowledge of more than some few veins, while, in order to obtain a true and perfect knowledge of these, I have dissected more than ten human bodies, destroying all the various members, and removing even the very smallest particles of the flesh which surrounded these veins, without causing any effusion of blood other than the imperceptible bleeding of the capillary veins. And as one single body did not suffice for so long a time, it was necessary to proceed by stages with so many bodies as would render my knowledge complete; and this I repeated twice over in order to discover the differences.

"But though possessed of an interest in the subject you may perhaps be deterred by natural repugnance, or, if this does not restrain you, then perhaps by the fear of passing the night hours in the company of these corpses, quartered and flayed and horrible to behold; and if this does not deter you then perhaps you may lack the skill in drawing essential for such representation; and even if you possess this skill it may not be combined with a knowledge of perspective, while, if it is so combined, you may not be versed in the methods of geometrical demonstration or the method of estimating the forces and strength of muscles, or perhaps you may be found wanting in patience so that you will not be diligent. Concerning which things, whether or no they have all been found in me, the hundred and twenty books which I

The requirement of "perspective," surprising to the modern reader at first glance, makes us see as in a flash that anatomy as a science (and this applies to all the other observational or descriptive disciplines) was simply not possible without a method of preserving observations in graphic records, complete and accurate in three dimensions.[29] In the absence of such records even the best observation was lost because it was not possible to check it against others and thus to test its general validity. It is no exaggeration to say that in the history of modern science the advent of perspective marked the beginning of a first period; the invention of the telescope and the microscope that of a second; and the discovery of photography that of a third: in the observational or descriptive sciences illustration is not so much the elucidation of a statement as a statement in itself.[30]

---

have composed will give their verdict 'yes' or 'no.' In these I have not been hindered either by avarice or negligence but only by want of time. Farewell!"

[29] Vangensten *et al.*, I, fol. 2; Richter, No. 798, here quoted after Heydenreich, p. 123 f.:

". . . if you wish to know thoroughly the parts of a man after he has been dissected you must either turn him or your eye so that you are examining from different aspects, from below, from above and from the sides, turning him over and studying the origin of each limb . . .

"Therefore by my plan you will become acquainted with every part and every whole by means of a demonstration of each part from three different aspects; for when you have seen any member from the front with the nerves, tendons and veins which have their origin on the opposite side, you will be shown the same member either from a side view or from behind, just as though you had the very member in your hand and went on turning it from side to side until you had a full understanding of all that you desire to know."

[30] The novelty and importance of Léonardo's achievement in using draftsmanship not as a means of illustrating a text (more often than not by simply repeating and often distorting an earlier drawing) but as a means of recording and transmitting new factual observations, so emphatically stressed by himself, has often been commented upon by

Even the best pre-Leonardesque *situs* pictures (that is to say, anatomical renderings of a woman in the state of pregnancy) are spooks and phantoms as compared to the famous Windsor drawing by Leonardo da Vinci (Fig. 9). And when we juxtapose this drawing with the equally famous woodcut (Fig. 10) in Vesalius' *Fabrica* of 1543 (or, for that matter, with any later parallel) it is apparent that a "mutational change" not only in presentation but also in essence has taken place in Leonardo. Far be it from me to side with those who make Vesalius a plagiarist. But it does not detract from his greatness to say that, while his *Fabrica* immeasurably surpasses Leonardo's fragmentary studies in completeness, systemtic organization and countless details, it does not essentially differ from it in purpose and method. And the objection that Leonardo's anatomical studies could not have been accessible to Vesalius can be disproved by the fact that

---

modern scholars; see, in addition to Heydenreich, p. 121 ff., the literature quoted in Note 26. Especially important are the following contributions: J. Lebengarc, "Ueber die Anatomie des Herzens in Leonardo da Vincis anatomischen Manuskripten," *Archiv für Geschichte der Medizin*, XVIII, 1926, p. 172 ff. (cf. K. D. Keele, *Leonardo da Vinci on Movement of the Heart and Blood*, London and Montreal, 1952); O. Benesch, "Leonardo da Vinci and the Beginning of Scientific Drawing," *The American Scientist*, XXXI, 1943, p. 311 ff.; Esche, *op. cit.*; R. Herrlinger, "Die didaktische Originalität der anatomischen Zeichnungen Leonardos," *Anatomischer Anzeiger*, XCIX, 1953, p.366 ff.; *idem*, "Katalog und Fragment." All authors agree that it was Leonardo who introduced, in addition to the correlation of perspective images with vertical and horizontal sections, the demonstration of the internal organs "in transparency" (we must be particularly grateful to Herrlinger for insisting that the illustrations in Magnus Hundt's *Antropologium*, published in 1501, are still entirely medieval in this respect whereas those in Lorenz Fries' *Spiegel der Artzeney*, published in 1517, already reveal the mutational change effected by Leonardo); the reduction of muscles to mere "strings" in order to clarify what may be called their topology; serial cross sections; and the exact definition of cavities by the injection method. For the latter two innovations, cf. below, Notes 33 and 35.

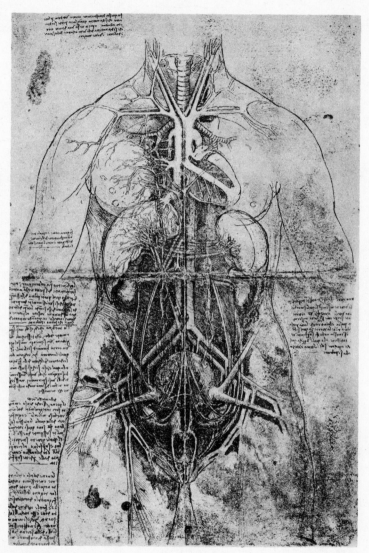

9. Leonardo da Vinci, *Situs* picture (Windsor Castle, Drawing No. 12283).

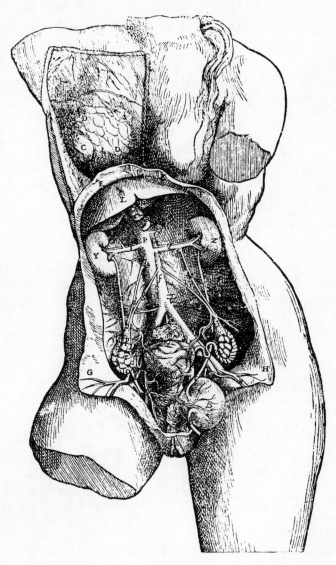

10. J. Stephan of Calcar, *Situs* picture from Andreas Vesalius, *De humani corporis fabrica*, Basel, 1543.

many of them, some now lost in the original, were copied in North Italy as late as about 1570.[31]

In the case of the embryo itself, the path of pictorial tradition can be traced back to a Late Antique treatise boldly ascribed to no less a personage than the midwife of Queen Cleopatra. But in its early medieval derivatives the embryos

[31] Vesalius' relationship to Leonardo needs restudying. E. Jackschath's attempt to make Vesalius a downright plagiarist of Leonardo (H. Cushing, *A Bio-Bibliography of Andreas Vesalius*, New York, 1943, p. xxxvii, p. 206, Nos. 211 and 212) has been generally and deservedly rejected (see, e.g., M. Holl, "Leonardo da Vinci und Vesal," *Archiv für Anatomie und Physiologie, anatomische Abteilung*, XXIX, 1905, p. 111 ff. [Cushing, No. 191]). But the similarities in representational technique, occasionally even in substantive content (cf. Sudhoff, "Tradition und Naturbeobachtung," p. 85 ff.), are too close to be accidental, and the Gordian knot cannot, I believe, be cut by the assumption that Leonardo's anatomical drawings, "hidden for hundreds of years," could not have been accessible to Vesalius while he was active in Italy. A number of anatomical drawings by Leonardo were copied by Dürer (see A. Weixlgärtner, "Die Vorlagen von Dürers anatomischen Studien in Dürers Dresdner Codex," *Mitteilungen der Gesellschaft für vervielfältigende Kunst* [*Die Graphischen Künste*, Supplement], XXXIX, 1906, p. 25 ff.; K. Sudhoff, "Dürers anatomische Zeichnungen in Dresden und Leonardo da Vinci," *Archiv für Geschichte der Medizin*, I, 1908, p. 317 ff.); a considerable number of other scientific drawings by Leonardo have come down to us—in part exclusively—through North Italian copies of the latter half of the sixteenth century (see, e.g., E. Panofsky, *The Codex Huygens and Leonardo da Vinci's Art Theory* [Studies of the Warburg Institute, XIII], London, 1940, pp. 41-58); and Vasari as well as Lomazzo were permitted to see "gran parte di queste carte della notomia degli uomini" in the house of Francesco Melzi, then a "bello e gentile vecchio," who was forty-five or forty-six when Vesalius appeared in North Italy in 1537. Quite apart from this, it is not too hazardous to presume that some of the anatomical studies made by Leonardo in collaboration with Marcantonio della Torre (for some bibliographical references, see W. von Seidlitz, *Leonardo da Vinci*, K. Zoege von Manteuffel, ed., Vienna, 1935, pp. 357 f., 531; Saxl, "Pagan Sacrifice," p. 356), or at least duplicates thereof, had remained in Marcantonio's possession and, after his death in 1511 or 1512, operated as another vehicle of transmission.

11. *Uterus Containing Embryos* (Brussels, Royal Library, MS. 3714, fol. 27v., Ninth Century).

look like diminutive adults, merrily disporting themselves in their schematized abode like Goethe's Homunculus in his glass bottle (Fig. 11). And so they continued to look in some charming drawings of the latter half of the fifteenth century, (Fig 12) and even in a German treatise of 1513 called *The*

Rose Garden.[32] But more than a decade before, Leonardo
had made a series of drawings which oppose truth to half a
thousand years of fiction and yet, as an art historian may be
permitted to add, not only defy the borderline between scientific illustration and "art" but mysteriously evoke that age-
old feeling, expressed by so many great poets, that life is
death and death is life (Fig. 13).

There is no need for further illustration of what Leonardo
meant in coining the phrase *pittore anatomista.* Suffice it to
say that in some cases the interpenetration of "scientific" and

12. *Uterus Containing Embryos* (Paris, Bibliothèque Nationale, MS.
lat. 7056, fol. 88, Drawings Added in the Fifteenth Century to a
Thirteenth-Century Manuscript).

"artistic" procedures can be observed even in purely technical
matters. Leonardo's "serial sections" (Fig. 14) represent a
concrete, surgical application of a method of geometrical pro-

[32] For the embryological representations here mentioned, see Sudhoff,
"Tradition und Naturbeobachtung," p. 69 ff.; and, more specifically,
idem, "Ein Beitrag zur Geschichte der Anatomie im Mittelalter,"
Studien zur Geschichte der Medizin, IV, 1908, p. 73 ff. (cf. also
A. A. Barb, *"Diva Matrix . . . ,"* *Studies of the Courtauld and
Warburg Institutes,* XVI, 1953, p. 193 ff.). The fifteenth-century
drawings referred to in the text (Paris, Bibliothèque Nationale, MS. lat.
7056, fols. 87v.-89) are illustrated by Sudhoff on Pl. XIX. Squeezed
into the lower margins of a thirteenth-century manuscript, they were,
in my opinion, added *ex post facto* to an originally unillustrated text.

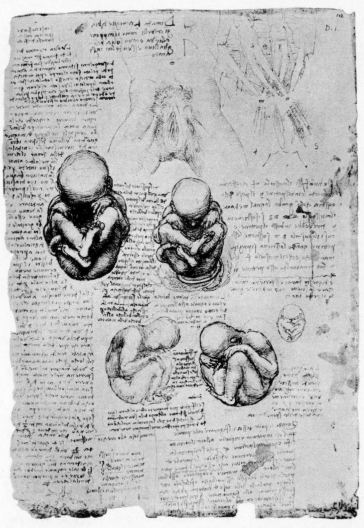

13. Leonardo da Vinci, *Embryo* (Windsor Castle, Drawing No. 19101).

14. Leonardo da Vinci, *Serial Sections of a Leg* (Windsor Castle, Drawing No. 12617).

jection developed by Piero della Francesca (Fig. 15) and later on adopted by Dürer: the plotting of a series of cross-sections through the human body preparatory to exact perspective construction.[33] And another, even more spectacular

[33] The didactic importance of serial sections is justly stressed by nearly all the authors cited in Notes 26 and 30, particularly by Belt, "Les Dissections," p. 208, and Herrlinger, "Die didaktische Originalität"; but it seems to have escaped notice that Leonardo's procedure derives from a device developed by the theorists of perspective who, in order to make the complex forms of the human body constructible according to Brunelleschi's "costruzione legittima," had to prepare a series of cross sections taken at various levels. The production and application of such "pre-anatomical serial sections"—showing, of course, only the outer contours, and not the interior structure, of the object—was taught by Piero della Francesca (*De prospectiva pingendi*, G. Nicco Fasola, ed., Florence, 1942) and was adopted and perfected by Dürer (Panofsky, *Dürers Kunsttheorie*, pp. 45-64). Our Fig. 15 is taken from Nicco Fasola's edition, Pl. XXXVI.

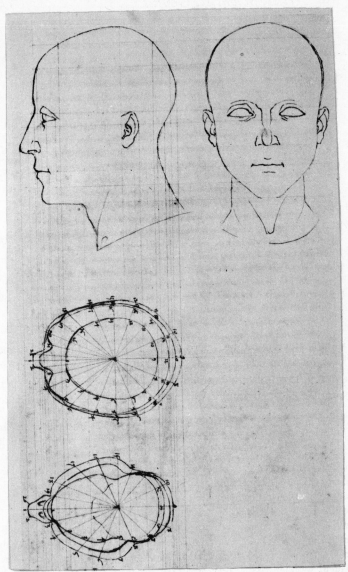

15. After Piero della Francesca, *Serial Sections of a Head Constructed in Preparation of Perspective Rendering* (Parma, Biblioteca Palatina, Cod. Cart 1576, fol. 59v.).

innovation in anatomical technique could have been devised only by a bronze sculptor.

From ancient times it was known that the human brain contains three cavities or ventricles, two of them so lobed that they could be thought of as divided into separate cells. And it was assumed that the anterior cavity was the seat of the *sensus communis* and/or imagination; the central one that of the cogitative faculty and/or judgment; and the posterior one that of memory (hence the phrase, "It is in the back of my head"). The exact topography of these ventricles remained, however, obscure. In medieval illustrations we either find the whole brain reduced to an abstract, geometrical diagram; or else we find the ventricles schematically entered into a fairly naturalistic head, originally represented in three-quarter view but later in full profile (Fig. 16). Towards 1500 the three-quarter view was reinstated, and in a remarkable woodcut of 1498 Dürer carried naturalism so far as to invest the *caput physicum*, as it was called, with the characteristic features of his friend Pirckheimer (Fig. 17). But this was a mere surface naturalism, the ventricles themselves remaining as schematic as ever. It was left to Leonardo (who in the field of brain anatomy has been found to be superior to even Vesalius)[34] to determine their size and shape experimentally (Fig. 18). He had the ingenious idea of draining them and then filling them with liquid wax, providing, exactly as in metal casting, two tiny tubes for the air to escape. When the wax had been allowed to harden, he could take as many accurate sections as he pleased.[35] And if this does not represent

[34] See M. Holl, "Vesals Anatomie des Gehirns," *Archiv für Anatomie und Physiologie, Anatomische Abteilung*, XXXIX, 1915, p. 115 f. (Cushing, No. 195).

[35] For Leonardo's method of wax injection and its originality, described in detail in Vangensten, *et. al., op. cit.*, V, 1916, fol. 7, see particularly Herrlinger, "Die didaktische Originalität"; Belt, "Les Dissections anatomiques," p. 208 f. (with reference to the fact that Leonardo applied the method not only to the cavities of the brain but also to those of the heart); O'Malley and Saunders, *op. cit.*, remarks

a transition from pre-scientific to scientific methods it is not easy to say what could.

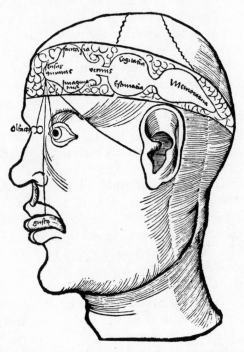

16. *Caput Physicum* (Woodcut from Gregorius Reisch, *Margarita Philosophica*, Strasbourg, 1504).

---

to Pl. 147 (Windsor 19127). While Galen is known to have inflated the cerebral vessels with air, nobody seems to have discovered the source of the assertion that solidifying injections into the blood vessels were used by Alessandro Giliani of Persicato (d. 1326). It is certain that liquid wax was first used by Leonardo and that this method was taken up by other anatomists, particularly Fredrik Ruysch (1638-1731), only in the seventeenth century. This makes it all the more probable that Leonardo applied a technique familiar to the sculptor but not to the

17. Albrecht Dürer, *Caput Physicum* (showing the features of Willibald Pirckheimer,
Woodcut Pass. 444, 1498).

medical man. For the representation of the cerebral ventricles before
Leonardo see W. Sudhoff, "Die Lehre von den Hirnventrikeln in
textlicher und graphischer Tradition des Mittelalters," *Archiv für
Geschichte der Medizin*, VII, 1913, p. 149 ff., particularly p. 204 ff.
While Leonardo radically broke with tradition as far as the physical structure of the brain is concerned he still accepted, to some extent, the
medieval theory according to which the ventricles were the *loci* of certain well-defined psychological faculties (cf. J. Leyacker, "Zur Entstehung der Lehre von den Hirnventrikeln als Sitz psychischer Vermögen,"
Archiv für Geschichte der Medizin, XIX, 1927, p. 253 ff.): in the very
drawing on which Leonardo describes his injection procedure and
records its spectacular results, the ventricles in the longitudinal section
are inscribed "imprensiva," "senso commune" and "memor[ia]," and
the caption identifies this drawing as "figura del senso commune gittato
di cera pel fondo pel la base del craneo pel buco . . ."

I have said that a perfectly good observation, made by a scientist, was bound to be lost as long as it could not be adequately recorded in an image. Conversely, as soon as art had reached the stage of adequate recording, a perfectly good observation, made by an artist, might be lost when it failed to be noticed by the scientists.

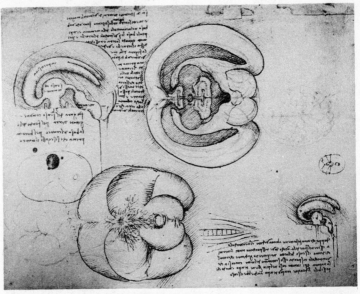

18. Leonardo da Vinci, *The Ventricles of the Brain, Their Form Established by the Injection Method* (Windsor Castle, Drawing No. 19127).

In a probably Spanish *Visitation* of *ca.* 1420 which, as was not unusual, reveals the Infant Jesus and the infant St. John within their mothers' wombs as in transparency, the embroiderer—or, as I prefer to think, embroideress—shows enough courage to represent the embryonic state of the children much more realistically than is the case in any professional medical illustration of the time (Fig. 19). From as early as about 1440, advanced Northern painters, such as Conrad Witz, proved themselves to be familiar with the optical law according to

19. *The Visitation* (Spanish [?] Embroidery, Cambridge, Mass., Fogg
Art Museum, Acqu. No. 1928.118 [detail], about 1420).

which the surface of a body of water no longer permits us to discern the objects beneath it, but reflects only the objects above it, as soon as the angle of incidence exceeds what is known as the critical value (Fig. 20); yet this law was not explicitly formulated in physics until the seventeenth century.

However, such "scientific discoveries out of context," as they might be called, would seem to be typical of the non-Italian world of the fifteenth century where no close contact existed between a painting enormously advanced in optical sensibility and technical refinement, and a science still fully medieval; and where, as Dürer acutely remarked, no bridge existed between "theory" (*Kunst*) and "practice" (*Brauch*). In Italy, as has been seen, science and art were decompartmentalized from the beginning of the Quattrocento, and we can even observe a characteristic tendency of scientists and artists to hunt in pairs, so to speak. Leonardo, the painter, needed Marcantonio della Torre, the professional anatomist, just as Vesalius, the professional anatomist, needed Stephan of Calcar, the marvelous woodcut designer.[36] Leonhard Fuchs,

[36] For the importance of Stephan of Calcar's participation in Vesalius' work, not only in the *Fabrica* of 1543 but also in the *Tabulae anatomicae sex* of 1538, where Calcar is even mentioned as publisher (*sumptibus*), see particularly W. M. Ivins, Jr., "The Woodcuts of Vesalius," *Bulletin of the Metropolitan Museum of Art*, XXXI, 1936, p. 139 ff., and the same author's even more important "A propos of the *Fabrica* of Vesalius," *Bulletin of the History of Medicine*, XIV, 1943, p. 576 ff. (Cushing, Nos. 209, 210). In support of the principle that "what can be shown cannot be said" (which naturally implies that what cannot be shown cannot be verified and, if necessary, corrected), Ivins points out that the text of the *Fabrica* was probably not written before the woodcuts (their blocks appropriated by Vesalius in somewhat irregular manner and used without due credit to the artist) were available; and that the beautiful postures of the skeletons at the beginning must be credited to Calcar's artistic imagination because the skeleton actually used by Vesalius and still preserved at Basel was immovable except for the jaw and the top of the head. It does not follow, however, that Calcar deserves more credit as an observer than Vesalius himself. That the wood blocks were cut before the text was written does not pre-

20. Conrad Witz, *St. Christopher* (Basel, Kunstmuseum).

the botanist, shared work and glory with his three illustrators, Veit Rudolf Specklin, Albrecht Meyer and Heinrich Füllmauer of whom even the portraits are included in Fuchs' *De historia stirpium,* the parent-work of scientific botany.[37] And as a last illustrious pair there may be mentioned Galileo and his faithful Lodovico Cigoli. Cigoli expertly assisted Galileo in his astronomical observations and in turn made use of them in his paintings. Thus, "as a good and loyal friend," he depicted the *Assunta* in the dome of the Papal Chapel in S. Maria Maggiore (completed in 1612) standing upon a moon which exhibits all the unexpected features recently revealed by Galileo's telescope: the "jagged dividing line" and

---

clude the fact that they were cut according to Vesalius' instructions; and that the breastbone in the *Tabulae* still consists of seven separate bones (a "Galenic error" corrected in the *Fabrica*) proves only that *both* Vesalius and Calcar were wrong in 1538, and right in 1543, but not that it was the latter rather than the former who discovered the truth. The same objection applies, *a fortiori,* to those "Galenic errors" which are perpetuated even in the illustrations of the *Fabrica,* first of all the non-existent perforations in the septum of the heart (cf. Note 19). For the quarrel between Vesalius and Calcar, which would seem to have occurred between 1539, when the former called the latter "the most admirable artist of our time" (Cushing, *op. cit.,* p. xxxviii), and the publication of the *Fabrica* in 1543, see G. Zilboorg, "Psychological Sidelights on Andreas Vesalius," *Bulletin of the History of Medicine,* XIV, 1943, p. 562 ff. (Cushing, No. 423). For the Titianesque character of Calcar's woodcuts, particularly evident in the landscapes behind the skeletons in the *Fabrica,* see E. Tietze-Conrat, "Neglected Contemporary Sources Relating to Michelangelo and Titian," *Art Bulletin,* XXV, 1943, p. 154 ff.

[37] For Leonhard Fuchs' *De historia stirpium commentarii insignes,* Basel, 1542, see, e.g., W. Blunt, *The Art of Botanical Illustration,* London, 1950, p. 48 ff., following an evalution of Leonardo's botanical drawings. As chance would have it, the German edition of Fuchs' highly successful work appeared as early as the following year— the same which saw the publication of Vesalius' *Fabrica* and Copernicus' *De revolutionibus orbium coelestium.*

21. Lodovico Cigoli, *Assunta* (Fresco, Rome, Santa Maria Maggiore, 1612).

the "little islands" which we call craters[38] (Fig. 21). In his
fresco the moon of Revelation:12 looks exactly like the moon
in Galileo's *Sidereus Nuncius*; and it is a nice piece of historical irony that the Chapel of Paul V should thus immortalize and magnify one of the very discoveries which,
through disproving the essential difference between the earth
and the celestial bodies, contributed so much to the defeat of
orthodox cosmology.

VI

To account for the many phenomena, some of which I have
tried to describe, one may point out a number of sociological
changes: the concentration of wealth, power and cultural
enterprise in the hands of an aristocratic elite as opposed to
communal organizations; the growing secularization of education; the formation of private groups and circles of *dilet-
tanti* (ultimately consolidated into "academies") interested in
all sorts of things; the concomitant disintegration of the
Guild System; and, as a result of all this, the new prestige of
the inventor, the military and civilian engineer and, quite particularly, the artist. In 1378 the painters of Florence were
granted the privilege of forming an independent branch
within the Doctors' and Apothecaries' Guild to which they
belonged because their work was "important for the life of
the state";[39] Giotto, a painter, was made the superintendent
of all artistic work connected with Florence Cathedral;[40]
Andrea Mantegna and Titian were ennobled; and the idea

[38] See E. Panofsky, *Galileo as a Critic of the Arts*, The Hague,
1954, p. 4 ff. (an abridged and revised reprint, entitled "Galileo as a
Critic of the Arts: Aesthetic Attitude and Scientific Thought," is found
in *Isis*, XLVII, 1956, p. 3 ff.).

[39] See M. Meiss, *Painting in Florence and Siena after the Black
Death*, Princeton, 1951, p. 63.

[40] See W. Paatz, "Die Gestalt Giottos im Spiegel einer zeitgenös-
sischen Urkunde," *Eine Gabe der Freunde für Carl Georg Heise zum
28.VI.1950*, Berlin, 1950, p. 85 ff.

that Michelangelo or Raphael should have belonged to a guild at all is almost ludicrous. Did not Dürer write from Venice in 1506: "How I shall long for the sun—here I am a gentleman, at home I am a parasite".[41]

However, the very personal tone of an utterance like this should warn us that, while it is true that the individual is a product of society, it is no less true that society is a product of individuals; and that, while a changing reality produces new ideas, a new idea may produce a change in reality. No one today would dare to take literally the fine old formula that the Renaissance meant the "*discovery* of the world and man." But it remains true that the *concept* of man—and, therefore, the *concept* of the world—did undergo a significant change in the Italian Quattrocento, and that this very change went a long way to abolish all those medieval partitions and boundaries.

Needless to say, the Middle Ages accepted as a basic tenet of Christianity the fact that man, created in the image of God, was free, that he was able to produce, and that he was an end rather than a means. But there is a world of difference between Brunetto Latini's "All things between heaven and earth were made for man but man was made for himself" (to which a pious annotator felt moved to add "and in order to live and serve God so as to attain to eternal bliss") and Pico della Mirandola's "Thou, man, masterful molder and sculptor of thyself ("tui ipsius arbitrarius plastes et fictor") may'st shape thyself into whichever form thou wantst."[42] There is a world of difference between man's freedom to accept or reject the Grace of God and his freedom to choose

---

[41] Letter to Pirckheimer of about October 13, 1506 (Lange and Fuhse, *op. cit.*, p. 41, line 4 f.): "O, wie wird mich nach der Sunnen frieren, hie bin ich ein Herr, doheim ein Schmarotzer."

[42] Both passages are reprinted in the Excursus No. LXXVIII in Jacob Burckhardt, *Die Kultur der Reinaissance* (10th edition, Leipzig, 1908, II, p. 314 f.; English edition available in Harper Torchbook series).

between his own, self-generated impulses; and it is this second kind of freedom which made possible the emergence of the two major literary forms which were virtually absent from the medieval scene: the novel (as opposed to the romance) and the drama (as opposed to the mystery play).

22. *Man between Angel and Devil* (South German Drawing, Basel, Kunstmuseum, about 1450).

The symbol of Latini's "man made for himself" is still Adam. The symbol of Pico's "man molding and sculpting himself" is Prometheus.[43] The medieval idea of freedom is visually expressed by a man torn between an angel and a devil (Fig. 22).[44] The Renaissance idea of freedom is visually

[43] See O. Raggio, "The Myth of Prometheus: Its Survival and Metamorphoses up to the Eighteenth Century," *Journal of the Warburg and Courtauld Institutes*, XXI, 1958, p. 44 ff.

[44] Cf. E. Panofsky, *Hercules am Scheidewege und andere antike Bildstoffe in der neueren Kunst* (Studien der Bibliothek Warburg,

expressed by a man taking his choice between Pleasure and Virtue, in other words, *Hercules at the Crossroads* (Fig. 23) —an eminently moral story ignored by the Middle Ages up to Petrarch because it was no more than an eminently moral story.[45] The medieval mind could not as yet accept one Virtue, which amounted to a perfection attainable in this world by the efforts of man, but only a plurality of virtues derived from and reflecting that perfection which is Christ.[46]

XVIII), Leipzig and Berlin, 1930, p. 151 ff., Fig. 103. St. Thomas, distinguishing between "acquired," "inborn" and "infused" virtues (the last-named being, of course, the three theological virtues of Faith, Hope and Charity), states that even the acquired and inborn virtues cannot be practiced without divine assistance (*Summa Theologiae*, I, 2, qu. 63, art. 1) and that the infused ones operate in us without our active participation though not without our consent (*ibidem*, qu. 55, art. 4, concl.): "Virtus infusa *causatur in nobis a Deo sine nobis agentibus*, non tamen sine nobis consentientibus, et sic est intelligendum quod dicitur: 'quam Deus in nobis sine nobis operatur.'" Even where he defends free will against St. Augustine's semi-Pelagianism (*Summa Theologiae*, I, 2, qu. 109, art. 2) St. Thomas is careful to restrict it. Even before the Fall, he says, man by himself could act only according to the acquired and inborn virtues but needed divine assistance (*auxilium divinum*) in order to act according to the infused ones. And after the Fall he cannot even live according to the former without the aid of God: "Unde mens hominis etiam sani non ita habet dominium sui actus, quin indigeat moveri a Deo; et multo magis liberum arbitrium hominis infirmi post peccatum, per quod impeditur a bono per corruptionem naturae."

[45] See, in addition to Panofsky, *Hercules*, T. E. Mommsen, "Petrarch and the Story of Hercules," *Journal of the Warburg and Courtauld Institutes*, XVI, 1953, pp. 178 ff., with the important proof that it was Petrarch who, as in so many other cases, reintroduced the classical motif of Hercules at the Crossroads into the literature of the Renaissance.

[46] The first post-classical representations of "Virtue in general," characteristically in the guise of Hercules, do not occur until 1300: probably in Giovanni Pisano's Pisa pulpit, and certainly in Francesco Barberino's "Documenti d'Amore" (see E. Panofsky, *Studies in Iconology*, New York, 1939, available in a Harper Torchbook edition, 1962, p. 157, Note 97), and Barberino is careful to point out that he could

23. Girolamo di Benvenuto, *Hercules at the Crossroads* (Venice, Cà d'Oro).

not find any earlier attempt to personify this *virtus generaliter sumpta*. More than one and a half centuries later, Filarete, unacquainted with Barberino, makes an analogous statement about a comprehensive personification devised by himself (see *Hercules am Scheidewege*, pp. 187 ff., Figs. 117-118): "et leggendo et domandando, se mai alcuno di questi avessi figurati immodo che in una figura comprendere si potesse l'uno essere il vitio et l'altra la virtù, io non o ancora trovato, che in una figura figurate fussono come impiù, come a dire le quattro virtù cardinali et le tre theologiche, et così i septe vitii principali, che chi a uno animale et chi a un altro et così ancora la virtù a varie figure asimigliate."

As the Middle Ages restricted man's power to mold himself, so did it restrict his power to mold his world. "Creatura non potest creare"—"the creature cannot create," says St. Augustine; for (again according to St. Augustine) "it is one thing to found and control that which is begotten out of the inmost and highest center of causes, which is the work of God alone, and quite another to perform, according to the faculties granted by Him, some outward operation which produces something at one time or another, in this way or that."[47]

We men of the twentieth century, surrounded by hats "created" by Lili Daché, lipsticks "created" by Helena Rubenstein, freshman courses in "creative writing" and progressive schools providing "creative play periods," no longer realize what it meant to transfer to human production the very verb of which St. Thomas untiringly affirms that it cannot be properly applied to any action other than that of God.[48] But this is precisely what the Renaissance did. Dürer credits the painter with what he calls the "marvelous" gift of "creating

[47] St. Augustine, *De Trinitate*, III, 9 (*Patrologia Latina*, XLII, col. 877).

[48] For a particularly incisive discussion see *Summa Theologiae*, I, qu. 45, art. 5. Modern authors are often not very careful in their translations and paraphrases of medieval texts referring to human as opposed to divine production. In her otherwise admirable *Study of the Bible in the Middle Ages* (second edition, New York, 1952, p. 15) Miss Beryl Smalley makes Theodore of Mopsuestia say that "man is God-like because he shares in the divine power to *create* by devising new combinations, as in constructing a ship, a house or a town." What the venerable Bishop really says (*Philopion*, VI, 14, reprinted in R. Devreesse, *Essai sur Théodore de Mopsueste*, Studi e Testi, CXLI, Città del Vaticano, 1948, p. 13) is that God granted to man the ability to imitate (μίμησις) His creation by producing such things as "houses, towns and ships which were not in existence before." He is careful to designate this derivative human activity by the verb ἐργάζεσθαι (to work out, to produce), as opposed to κτίζειν (to create), and he especially points out that creation in this sense, viz., in the sense of calling into being something out of nothing, was a privilege of God alone: ἅπερ οὖν πρόδεστι τῷ δημιουργῷ τῶν ἁπάντων. Cf. also Note 52.

in his heart" what had never been in anyone's mind before; and he adds a statement which seems self-evident to us but "strange," even subversive to himself: "Therefore a man may sketch something with his pen on half a sheet of paper in one day, or cut it into a tiny piece of wood with his little iron, and it turns out to be better and more artistic than another's big work at which he has labored for a whole year."[49] And an English art critic of the sixteenth century says: "The very poet makes like God who, without any trauell to his diuine imagination, made the world out of nought, nor also by any patterne or mould."[50]

A man so gifted is indeed no longer human but "divine"; and *divino* was the epithet applied to Michelangelo by his contemporaries and to a host of lesser practitioners thereafter, down to the diva of the operatic stage. The rise of man to the status of "genius," however, was in a sense a second Fall from Grace. As his ambition for the "knowledge of good and evil" had brought upon him mortality and subjection to sin, so did his ambition for "creativeness" entail a threat to his sanity. The concept of genius was developed in the context of that Neoplatonic philosophy which has been mentioned before. Extending the prerogative of the saint and the prophet to the philosopher, the poet, and finally the artist, this doctrine accounted for the superhuman achievements of these secular geniuses by an inspiration from on high which produced—or,

[49] Lange and Fuhse, *op. cit.*, p. 297, line 27 ff.; pp. 295, line 8 ff.; p. 221, line 1 ff. Cf. Panofsky, *Albrecht Dürer*, I, p. 282 ff.; *idem, Idea, Ein Beitrag zur Begriffsgeschichte der älteren Kunsttheorie* (Studien der Bibliothek Warburg, V), Leipzig and Berlin, 1924 (second edition, Berlin, 1960), p. 68 ff.

[50] George (and/or Richard) Puttenham, *The Arte of English Poesie*, London, 1589, as quoted in M. C. Nahm, *The Artist as Creator: An Essay in Human Freedom*, Baltimore, 1956, p. 71 ff. An entirely new light on the problem has been thrown by E. H. Kantorowicz, "The Sovereignty of the Artist: A Note on Legal Maxims in Renaissance Art," *De Artibus Opuscula XL: Essays in Honor of Erwin Panofsky*, New York, 1961, p. 267 ff.

put it the other way, presupposed—what Plato had called "divine madness." And this *furor divinus* was linked, on the basis of a half-forgotten Aristotelian treatise, to that sublime and terrifying thing which elevates the genius beyond all ordinary mortals but also threatens him with tragedies unknown to them: melancholy. This melancholy, without which no one could be considered a genius from *ca.* 1500, places the "creative mind" on a dizzy height where he is lonely at best and from which he may tumble into the abyss of insanity at worst.[51]

Curiously enough, it was in the North rather than in Italy that this idea of genius was first applied to the visual arts. Leonardo da Vinci still assiduously avoids the word *creare* even where he asserts that the painter is "master and god" of a whole world of beauty and ugliness, mirth and sorrow; it was left to an annotator of *ca.* 1550 (the time when Michelangelo was commonly called *divino*) to explain Leonardo's phrase *signore e dio* as *creatore*.[52] But this time lag can be

---

[51] Since the publication of E. Panofsky and F. Saxl, *Dürers "Melencolia I," Eine quellen-und typengeschichtliche Untersuchung* (Studien der Bibliothek Warburg, II), Leipzig and Berlin, 1923, the literature concerning melancholy, Saturn and genius has increased to almost unmanageable proportions. Some references (see also Panofsky, *Albrecht Dürer*, third edition, Princeton, 1948, II, pp. 26, 170; fourth edition, Princeton, 1954, p. 301) will be given if and when the new English edition of our book is published.

[52] Leonardo da Vinci, *Trattato della Pittura* (Vatican Library, cod. Urb. 1270, fol. 5, reproduced in facsimile in A. Philip McMahon, tr. and ed., *Leonardo da Vinci, Treatise on Painting*, Vol. II): ". . . ne è signore e dio [corrected into *creatore* by "Hand 3"] et se uol generare siti, e deserti . . ." In McMahon's translation (Vol. II, p. 24) the word *generare*, occurring three times on the same page, is invariably rendered by "creating" or "to create." The same liberty has been taken in other places, for example, on p. 12, where even the word *operatione*, found on fol. 19v., is translated as "creative action"; I. Richter, *Paragone; A Comparison of the Arts by Leonardo da Vinci*, London, New York and Toronto, 1949, p. 21, even has "act of creation." The only occurrence in Leonardo's writings of the word *creazione* with reference

explained by the fact that the Italian Quattrocento had conducted the fight for social and intellectual recognition of the visual arts under the flag of science rather than "creativeness." The earlier art theorists, men like Alberti, Ghiberti and Piero della Francesca, were no more concerned with influences from on high than the earlier Neoplatonists were with the visual arts, and Leonardo, attempting to prove that painting was a *scienza,* anticipated Galileo in maintaining that mathematics, and only mathematics, permitted the mind to attain incontrovertible certainty.

In the North, however, where no art theory existed before Dürer, the influence of Alberti, Piero della Francesca and Leonardo arrived simultaneously with that of Marsilio Ficino, and these two currents interpenetrated at once. As early as 1509 Agrippa of Nettesheim claimed the privilege of original invention induced by divine (or melancholy) inspiration, which the Florentine Academy had reserved to those who had expressed themselves in words, for the practitioners of

---

to artistic activity appears to be a "ghost." According to E. Cassirer, *Individuum und Kosmos in der Philosophie der Renaissance* (Studien der Bibliothek Warburg, X, 1927), p. 170; Italian translation, Florence, 1955, p. 255 (English translation to be published by Harper & Row in 1963), Leonardo is said to have written: "La scienza è una seconda creazione fatta col discorso, la pittura è una seconda creazione fatta colla fantasia." But in spite of the expert help generously offered by Professor L. H. Heydenreich, Mrs. Kate Steinitz and Dr. Carlo Pedretti, I have been unable to locate this passage (also suspect by the use of the word *fantasia*) and agree with Professor Heydenreich's suggestion that Cassirer, quoting from memory, reproduced a modern paraphrase of Leonardo's views rather than an authentic text. In the captions in E. Solmi's useful little anthology *Leonardo da Vinci, Frammenti letterari e filosofici,* Florence, 1908, for example, we find such phrases as "La Pittura è una seconda Creazione." Cassirer's persuasive formula has subsequently found its way into J. Babini, "Leonardo, Teorico del arte y de la ciencia," *Sur, Revista Mensual,* Buenos Aires, November-December 1952, p. 34 ff., especially p. 39.

the visual arts.[53] In 1532, the Dutch painter, Maerter van Heemskerck, represented St. Luke portraying the Virgin Mary from life but guided and illumined by the ivy-wreathed *Furor poeticus* (Fig. 24). And eighteen years before, Dürer himself had condensed into the magnificent symbol of his *Melencolia I* (Fig. 25) the whole predicament of a mind which deeply felt, but was as yet unable to resolve, the tension between scientific truth (Dürer, like Leonardo and Galileo, believed that only mathematics could provide certainty but wistfully added that there were many things beyond the reach of it)[54] and the Neoplatonic gospel of super-rational inspiration.

This tension turned into open conflict by the end of the sixteenth century when such art theorists as Raffaele Borghini, Gregorio Comanini and Federico Zuccari attacked mathematics as an enslavement of the spirit; and when the value of all rational rules was verbally challenged in the name of divine madness and heroic furors ("There are as many rules as there are true poets," says Giordano Bruno)[55] and visibly denied by Caravaggio's new naturalism. The time had come for another compartmentalization, for the drawing of new boundaries which were to prove valid, more or less, up to our own day. It was realized that the numerous planes which the Renaissance had projected onto one surface were, in fact, distinct and had to be separated again—according to principles which could become evident only once the projection had been performed.

[53] See, for the time being, Panofsky, *Albrecht Dürer*, I, pp. 168 ff., 281 f.

[54] Lange and Fuhse, *op. cit.*, p. 363, line 5 ff. (quoted, e.g., in Panofsky and Saxl, *Dürers "Melencolia,"* p. 75).

[55] For this "anti-rational" trend in Mannerist art theory see Panofsky, *Idea*, p. 41 ff. For authors holding views similar to those of Zuccari and Giordano Bruno, particularly Francesco Patrizi in *Della Poetica* (1586), cf. the interesting essay by S. H. Monk, "A Grace beyond the Reach of Art," *Journal of the History of Ideas*, V, 1944, p. 131 ff.

24. Martin van Heemskerck, *St. Luke Portraying the Madonna* (Haarlem, Frans Hals Museum, 1532).

25. Albrecht Dürer, *Melencolia I* (Engraving B.74, 1514).

Thus science, purified of all magical and mystical connotations, emerged as the strictly quantitative interpretation of nature which we accept it to be and therefore parted company with humanistic scholarship, philosophy and art. Humanistic scholarship, philosophy and art in turn parted company with science. Descartes' and Désargues' mathematics, not to

26. Pietro da Cortona, detail from ceiling in Palazzo Barberini (Rome, 1633-1639).

mention that of Fermat, outgrew the realm of visual applicability, and the very fact that the world of observational science was increasingly dominated by telescopic and microscopic instrumentation served to estrange it from the world of the artist. Normally the painters painted what could be discerned with the naked eye.[56] They had few occasions to

[56] The new dissociation of art from science in the seventeenth century has been dealt with by Professor James S. Ackerman, "Science and Visual Art," in *Seventeenth Century Science and the Arts*, ed. by H. Rhys, Princeton, 1961, p. 63 ff.

represent the moon according to Galileo, and when Pietro da Cortona had to enlarge the heraldic bees of his patrons to the heroic scale in which they appear on the ceiling of the Palazzo Barberini (Fig. 26), he preferred to represent them in their traditional form instead of exploiting the earliest microscopic design to appear in a printed book, the beautiful etching in Francesco Stelluti's translation of Persius (Fig. 27), although this precious little volume had appeared only three years before the painter began to work on the ceiling and had been dedicated to Francesco Cardinal Barberini, a nephew of Maffeo Barberini who was then "ruling the world" as Pope Urban VIII.[57]

Even within the sciences the process of separation started all over again. Physics is now divided into theoretical and experimental physics, and humanistic scholarship has managed to crystallize into such well-defined "disciplines" as philology, archaeology, numismatics, political history, diplomatics or, for that matter, the history of art. There is, however, this difference between compartmentalization before and after the great decompartmentalization of the Renaissance: every hypothesis evolved by the theoretical physicist is tested by new experiments while new experiments can, and often do, suggest new theories (it would no longer be possible to discuss the acceleration of free-falling bodies on purely logical grounds). And even the humanists have developed rules of evidence no less strict than those for science, with the result that in our century the art historian, the archaeologist, the numismatist and the diplomatist must rely not only on each other but very often must also call to their rescue the zoologist, the botanist,

[57] Francesco Stelluti, *Persio tradotto in verso sciolto e dichiarato*, Rome, 1630, fol. 51 f. The "Description of the Bee" (fols. 51-54v.) is appended to the translation of the First Satire, and its inclusion is justified in a long footnote on fol. 46v.: the bee is both the heraldic animal of the Barberini family and a symbol of the *studiosi* working under their protection, particularly the members of the Accademia dei Lincei, of which Stelluti was a co-founder, and the prime mover of which, Federico Cesi, had also written about bees, though only briefly and without illustrations.

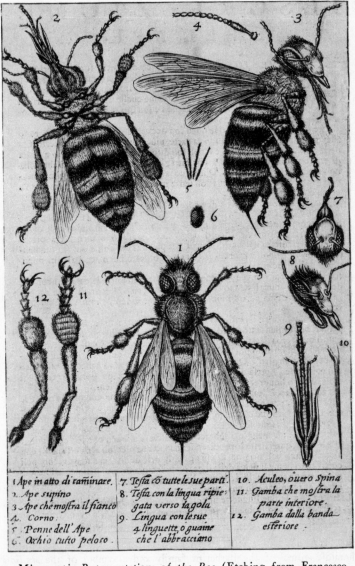

1 Ape in atto di caminare.	7. Testa cõ tutte le sue parti.	10. Aculeo, ouero Spina
2. Ape supino	8. Testa con la lingua ripie-	11. Gamba che mostra la
3. Ape che mostra il fianco	gata verso la gola	parte interiore.
4. Corno.	9. Lingua con le sue	12. Gamba dalla banda
5. Penne dell'Ape	4 linguette, o guaine	esteriore.
6. Occhio tutto peloso.	che l'abbracciano	

27. *Microscopic Representations of the Bee* (Etching from Francesco Stelluti, *Persio tradotto in verso sciolto e dichiarato*, Rome, 1630, p. 52).

the chemist and, above all, the radiologist.

Yet the fact remains that what had been a unity in the Renaissance is now, again, a complex diversity; and there are those who were not, are not, and will never be satisfied with this state of affairs. There is a type of mind, and not necessarily of an inferior order, which finds it impossible to accept the sum of parts as a substitute for the whole, the quantitative as a substitute for the qualitative, a series of equations as a substitute for significance; and there is no denying that the reduction of nature to a system of numerical relations, so uncompromisingly demanded and put into practice by Galileo, was bound to leave a kind of psychological vacuum.

We may laugh at a man like Francesco Sizi who attempted to disprove the existence of the Jupiter satellites on the grounds that the assumption of more than seven planets was incompatible with the sacred nature of this number and would destroy a harmony ordained by God. And we may smile, respectfully, at Goethe, who refused to accept the results of Newton's optical experiments and held that the use of microscopes and telescopes merely "confuses the mind."[58] But it is more difficult to smile at Kepler, one of the chief architects of the new universe who, in contrast to Galileo, was not as yet prepared to bid goodby to the old. He rejected a perfectly plausible astronomical hypothesis because it was inaccurate by eight minutes; but he refused to abandon astrology. He found the three planetary laws which in sheer beauty are rivalled only by Newton's Law of Gravity; but he would have been unhappy had he not found a consonance between the structure of the physical world and the Trinity. When attacked by Robert Fludd, a visionary Rosicrucian who, like all mystics, hated the very idea of measurement and believed that the secrets of the cosmos could be penetrated only by inspired intuition, Kepler replied: "You may embrace the head [of the

[58] "Mikroskope und Fernröhre verwirren eigentlich den reinen Menschensinn" (Goethe, *Maximen und Reflexionen*, Jubiläums-Ausgabe, IV, p. 229).

universe] but you do so only in your mind, nay, in your dreams; I have merely the tail, but that I hold in my hand."[59] But he himself never could rid himself of animistic and numerological notions and found the "ideas of natural things" in geometrical figures. To a sober-minded surgeon he wrote: "I too, to be sure, am playing with symbols—in such a way, however, that I never forget that I am playing;"[60] but he never gave up the play.

The modern scientist can, of course, not think of reverting to Kepler; but he may well be sensitive to the loss entailed by what may be called the "re-compartmentalization" of the seventeenth century.

Let me conclude by quoting a theoretical physicist who has received a Nobel Prize for one of the most significant contributions after Planck and Einstein yet, characteristically, thought it worth his while to devote a penetrating study to the controversy between Kepler and Fludd just alluded to: "Though we now have natural sciences, we no longer have a total scientific picture of the world. Since the discovery of the quantum of action, physics has gradually been forced to relinquish its proud claim to be able to understand, in principle, the *whole* world. This very circumstance, however, as a correction of earlier one-sidedness, could contain the germ of progress toward a unified conception of the entire cosmos of which the natural sciences are only a part."[61]

[59] *Apologia adversus demonstrationem analyticam Roberti de Fluctibus* (*Johannis Kepleri opera omnia*, Chr. Frisch, ed., Frankfort, 1858, V, p. 460; *Gesammelte Werke*, M. Caspar, ed., Munich, 1938 ff., VI, p. 446): "Caudam ego teneo sed manu, tu caput amplectaris mente, modo ne somnians."

[60] Letter to Joachim Tanck of May 12, 1608 (Frisch, *op. cit.*, I, p. 378; Caspar, *op. cit.*, XVI, p. 158): "Ludo quippe et ego symbolis . . . : sed ita ludo, ut me ludere non obliviscar."

[61] W. Pauli, "The Influence of Archetypal Ideas on the Scientific Theories of Kepler," in C. G. Jung and W. Pauli, *The Interpretation of Nature and the Psyche* (Bollingen Series, LI), New York, 1955, p. 147 ff.; the passage quoted, p. 209.

INDEX